The Gardener's Guide
to Growing
CANNAS

The Gardener's Guide to Growing

CANNAS

Ian Cooke

David & Charles

TIMBER PRESS
Portland, Oregon

PICTURE CREDITS

Plates by Karl Adamson, photographs by Ian Cooke pp.16, 17, 18, 41, 42, 49, 74, 75, 76, 81, 90, 92, 98, 100, 104, 105, 106, 111, 112, 115, 116, 123, 124, 126, 136, 138, 139, 142 149, all other photographs by Justyn Willsmore.

NOTE

Throughout the book the time of year is given as a season to make the reference applicable to readers all over the world. In the northern hemisphere the seasons may be translated into months as follows:

Early winter	December	*Early spring*	March	*Early summer*	June	*Early autumn*	September
Midwinter	January	*Mid-spring*	April	*Midsummer*	July	*Mid-autumn*	October
Late winter	February	*Late spring*	May	*Late summer*	August	*Late autumn*	November

First published in the UK in 2001 by David & Charles Publishers,
Brunel House, Newton Abbot, Devon
ISBN 0 7153 1131 X

First published in North America in 2001 by Timber Press Inc.,
133 SW Second Avenue, Suite 450, Portland, Oregon 97204, USA
ISBN 0-88192-513-6

A catalog record of this book is available from the Library of Congress.

Designed and edited by Jo Weeks
Illustrated by Coral Mula
Printed in Italy by Stige

page 1   *Canna* 'Champigny'.

page 2   *Canna* 'Indica Purpurea' among bedding plants at Osborne House on the Isle of Wight.

page 3   *Canna* 'Pretoria'.

CONTENTS

AN INTRODUCTION TO CANNAS

Big, brash, bright and gaudy, cannas could be described as the clowns of the plant world. Most are not discreet; they flaunt their big floppy leaves in the breeze, and their huge flashy flowers stand proud and bold at the top of giant ramrod stems. Cannas are not for the faint-hearted! But it is for these flamboyant characteristics that the hot-headed among the gardening fraternity will choose them.

The description above is, of course, a generalization and among the members of this variable genus are also found delicate flowers, pastel shades and compact, well-behaved plants that would also suit the most refined and restrained gardening tastes.

If we could take a time-machine back a hundred years, we would find that cannas were highly fashionable and widely grown in both large and small gardens. Times and fashions changed and they lost their appeal but once again they have regained their popularity and are now talked about and grown by keen gardeners in many countries. Their exotic foliage and multi-coloured flowers have awarded them a new and well-deserved status as easy garden plants with instant appeal.

The name is derived from the Greek *kanna*, meaning a reed-like plant. Cannas are sometimes referred to as 'canna lilies', although they have no relationship to the lily family: the word is merely used here to suggest a large, exotic-looking flower. The other common name, occasionally used, is 'Indian shot plant', referring to the round, hard, black seeds that the plant produces. I have never been able to verify whether

The gaudy orange flowers of 'Durban' are an added bonus to the brilliant foliage.

they have ever been employed as missiles, but I believe that the seeds are used as rosary beads in Spain and Portugal. I have also heard of them being used as the contents for a Zimbabwean musical instrument, called a 'hosha', which is shaken.

Cannas suffer from a widespread misapprehension that they are difficult to grow. I have been at plant sales and witnessed ignorant but outspoken people dismissing them with a single cutting phrase, such as 'You can't grow those, they are tropical', and I have then seen a queue of potential customers melt away! However, nothing could be further from the truth.

Cannas *are* tropical plants, essentially natives of the West Indies and subtropical areas such as South America, where they are found in both mountainous and lowland areas. However, as ornamentals, they have been developed mainly in the temperate climate of Europe. As such, they have, over the years, been selected to be tolerant of a wide range of conditions and, provided a few basic requirements are understood, they are easy and rewarding to grow. As a generalization, they respond well to conditions and cultivation techniques that are similar to those required by dahlias. In fact I have often said that they are easier than dahlias as they do not require staking.

THE RANGE

The colour spectrum for modern cannas extends from deepest blood-reds, through pinks, salmons and lollipop-oranges to yellows and pale primrose. There are even some, such as 'Eureka', that claim to be white, although these are generally pale yellow fading to cream. The flowers may be spotted, blotched, streaked or flushed with another colour, most com-

The pink flowers of 'Shenandoah', an old nineteenth-century cultivar, tone well with C. *iridiflora* 'Ehemanii'.

monly red. Flowers vary in size from the diminutive blossoms of the species such as C. *indica*, through to the huge blowsy blooms of cultivars such as the orange 'Wyoming'. Some cultivars, including the cherry-red 'Strasbourg', have upright, almost iris-like flowers. Other flower shapes are big and open or narrow petalled and spidery, while some even resemble butterflies, orchids or funnels.

In height cannas vary from dwarfs, such as 'Lucifer' at a well-behaved 45cm (18in), to giants like C. 'Musifolia' at 2.1m (7ft), grown for its huge banana-like leaves.

Although many are green-leaved, there are some cannas with coloured foliage. The old nineteenth-century cultivar 'Shenandoah' has purple leaves that act as a handsome foil for its rich pink flowers. Then

there is C. *glauca*, a tall, elegant plant with pale yellow flowers and narrow blue-grey foliage. By contrast, the brash 'Pretoria' is a real love-it-or-hate-it plant with big bright green leaves, ferociously striped in yellow and crowned with hefty orange blooms. Other coloured-leaved cultivars include the brilliantly coloured 'Durban', which originated in South Africa a few years ago. Its purple- and pink-striped leaves are a kaleidoscopic and spectacular colour blend. 'Durban' grows to 1.5m (5ft) and freely produces huge, in-your-face orange flowers. Identical cultivars called 'Phasion' and 'Tropicanna'™ have recently appeared. The shorter-growing 'Pink Sunburst' is more refined with its pale pink flowers borne over purple leaves that are striped with cream. 'Stuttgart' grows to 2.1m (7ft) and has sophisticated narrow foliage, irregularly splashed with grey and white. It needs to be grown in light shade and with plenty of moisture to avoid the leaves being scorched.

A range of delicate plants, bred from C. *glauca*, have been dubbed 'water cannas' because of their ability to grow as marginals in shallow water. They are, however, good for borders, provided that they are not in dry soil. 'Taney' is a soft orange, 'Endeavour', red, 'Erebus', pale pink and 'Ra', a lemon-yellow. They are all tall and graceful with glaucous, lance-shaped foliage, like the species, and make an agreeable contrast to many other cannas.

There are no cannas that can be distinguished as having double flowers (multiple petals), although some have a fullness that gives the impression of being double. Botanically, the flower could be said to be double as the stamens are actually petaloid but more about that later (pp.22–29). Double mutants have been caused by irradiation but none of these have proved stable, or ornamental.

As with numerous other plants, breeding targets focus on producing cultivars that are easily sold in garden centres. This means that they need to be early flowering and short in stature. While the former characteristic is most certainly a benefit, particularly in climates with a brief summer season, the latter would seem to negate one of the main values of the canna: little squat plants have no grandeur or stature and become no more than a blob of amorphous colour, like so many other modern bedding plants. However, that is a personal opinion and, in their defence, it should be stated that some of the newer dwarf types do provide a splendid display and have many other very refined characteristics, such as the ability to drop their old flowers cleanly.

THIS BOOK

This book is for all those interested in growing cannas. It is intended as a practical guide and as such is for hands-on gardeners and for those with a love of plants. Within it there is sufficient information to enable the beginner to grow cannas successfully and also for the more experienced grower to further his or her knowledge. Hopefully, it will also be a reference document and in particular the descriptions of species and cultivars will be of value in identifying cannas and providing information on their background. To my knowledge, this book is the only comprehensive work published on cannas since 1903 and as such it marks the revival of interest in these magnificent plants.

In carrying out research for the book, I have become increasingly aware that this is a vast subject and that my experience is limited. Cannas are grown in many different countries, and it is inevitable that the techniques used for growing them, particularly in the area of overwintering, vary considerably with the climate. My primary experience has been gained from growing cannas in the British Isles and so, naturally, the main thrust of my advice relates to temperate climates; however, reference is also made to cultivation in warmer climates, which is intended to make the book of use across the USA and elsewhere.

Finally, there is the minefield of plant naming, which I shall discuss in more detail later. Here it is enough to state that, without extensive trials and research, which are not feasible for a book of this nature, I think it is not possible to solve some of the naming problems.

1

A HISTORY OF CANNAS

Cannas have been cultivated in one way or another for several centuries. For example, the *Florilegium Renovatum*, published in 1612, contains a copperplate illustration of *C. indica* and John Parkinson's *Flower Garden*, published in 1629, describes cultural techniques for cannas. However, the most interesting part of their history occurred in the second half of the nineteenth century. Over less than fifty years, cannas were transformed. At the beginning of this period, they were obscure tropical plants – tall, long-jointed and small-flowered. By the end of it, the hybrid canna had appeared: it is, by comparison, dwarf in habit with large, bold inflorescences of large, highly coloured flowers.

Part of the reason for this change was that it was found that cannas adapted well to culture in temperate climates. They rapidly gained popularity and became the height of horticultural fashion, being written about in many of the important journals of the day. They were planted in the most up-to-date gardens, and displayed at garden shows and exhibitions. Many of the most respected nurseries of the time grew at least some cannas, and many hybridists dabbled in producing new cultivars. Interest in them spread from France, through Europe, to the USA, India and many other countries. In his *American Flower Garden Directory* (1845), Robert Buist wrote that there were about 30 species, several of them deserving cultivation for both flower and foliage. He refers to *C. gigantea* as being the finest, with large leaves and orange flowers. He also enthused about *C. limbata*, *C. discolor* and *C.*

Few would realise that the modern, large-flowered cannas orginated from simple species such as *C. indica*.

iridiflora (many of these species names are no longer recognized, see pp.54–61).

CANNAS IN FRANCE

Some of the earliest collecting and hybridization of cannas was done by M. Thré Année in France. He had been French consular agent in Valparaiso, Chile and, during his travels in South America, had collected various wild species. On his return to France he started breeding cannas in his garden at Passy near Sens in northern France.

Starting in 1848, Année worked with *C. indica* (at the time misidentified as *C. nepalensis*) which he is thought to have crossed with *C. glauca* and other species. His early hybrids were mostly tall, probably well over 3m (10ft) high, and were grown primarily for their highly coloured foliage, which varied from green to red-purple. The flowers were salmon-yellow or orange-yellow and were no bigger than the species types. Nevertheless, these hybrids soon became popular and were widely grown by the middle of the nineteenth century. It is reported that 20,000 'tufts' of a canna called 'Annaei' were used in displays in Paris in 1861. Année continued work on his hybrids using *C. discolor* (*C.* 'Discolor'), which was short and had brighter red flowers.

Old lists contain reference to many cultivars that originated from Année's hybridization, including *C. Annei-rosea*, *Annei-marginata* and *Annei-rubra*. The spelling of the names is variable making verification difficult, and it is unlikely that any of these early hybrids is still available today. In the British Isles, the 1870 catalogue of nurseryman Rollison lists some 20 or so species and primary hybrids with the comment that they had been selected from continental lists of 100–150 varieties, where their popularity was already established. In 1871, Edward Sprague Rand of Boston, Massachusetts, USA referred to cannas in *Seventy Five Popular Flowers*, stating that 'No plant is more effective in the garden than the canna'. Among the plants he listed was C. *Anneii*, one of Année's first hybrids and his book also contains the earliest mention of C. *musaefolia* (C. 'Musifolia'), even today one of the best foliage types.

CROZY

Another Frenchman, M. Crozy of Lyons, started breeding cannas around the 1870s. His first hybrid, C. 'Bonnetti', was produced from C. *warszewiczii* (C. 'Warszewiczii') crossed with C. *nepalensis* 'Grandiflora'. Much more notable was C. 'Madame Crozy', produced in 1870 and described thus: 'brilliant orange-scarlet, edged with gold; large flowers and good, sturdy habit; fine for pots or bedding; height about three feet'.

'Madame Crozy' was the first of a whole new race of dwarf cannas. Crozy is believed to have produced it by crossing C. *iridiflora* with C. *warszewiczii*, which produced C. 'Ehemannii', which was then back-crossed to C. *warszewiczii*. The red colouring of 'Madame Crozy' originates from C. *warszewiczii*. Crozy included C. *glauca* in his breeding programme to add yellow to his range of dwarf hybrids, and from these basic species and the subsequent hybrids, he produced a wide palette of colours. He also selected for hardiness, to produce plants that would thrive in the open in the tougher climate of Europe.

For many years, these dwarf cannas were known as French cannas or gladiolus-flowered cannas, because of their similarity to gladiolus flowers. With sturdy flower stems, a long flowering season and large blooms, they were a tremendous improvement over the Année cannas and offered considerable novelty value at the time. Although, by the standards of the age, they were considered compact and were particularly recommended for bedding and pot culture, today we would think them quite tall.

Crozy was a prodigious breeder and by the time he was able to offer 'Madame Crozy' commercially, he already had a further 1,500 seedlings from it under trial! His catalogue for 1895 listed 20 quite new culti-

vars of his own raising, together with a further 220 other cultivars. Crozy was so well known for his plants in his home area, that he was called 'Papa Canna', a name also used for one of his hybrids.

In 1888, the Royal Horticultural Society awarded seven of Crozy's cannas First Class Certificates (FCC), a valued honour at the time. Many of his cultivars are now lost but 'Brilliant', 'Centenaire de Rozain-Boucharlat', 'Madame Paul Casaneuve' and 'Florence Vaughan' are still available, the latter two still being among the best of their type.

ON DISPLAY

Cannas had long had a part in public plantings in France. Victor Hugo had drawn special attention to them in the gardens of the 1868 Paris exhibition. In the later exhibition of 1890, many of Crozy's hybrids were planted in the display beds. At around the time of Crozy's death in 1903, Barrilet-Deschamp was influential in his use of tropicals such as cannas, coleus, caladium, dieffenbachia, philodendron and bananas in the bedding schemes in the Paris parks.

VILMORIN-ANDRIEUX

Mention should be made of the venerable French nursery firm of Vilmorin-Andrieux. One of the earliest of their introductions was 'Sémaphore', 1895, which is fairly unique in that it is one of very few yellows with bronze foliage. 'Assaut', 'En Avant', 'Hercule', 'La Gloire', 'Madame Angele Martin', 'Oiseau d'Or', and 'Oiseau de Feu', from the same nursery, were all produced in the twentieth century and are still widely grown today. The nursery's catalogue for 1910–11 lists 102 cultivars, with 'Oiseau de Feu' as their new introduction.

CANNAS IN ITALY

One of the next major breakthroughs in canna breeding occurred in the 1890s at the hands of M. Sprenger, a partner in the nursery of MM Dammann near Naples. Convinced that there was a need for new genetic material, now an established breeding technique, he introduced C. *flaccida*, a yellow-flowered species, from the southern USA. With this he hoped to increase hardiness and introduce a different-shaped flower to his breeding programme. After an unsuccessful start, he crossed C. *flaccida* with 'Madame Crozy' and, in 1893, from among a thousand seedlings, he selected a cultivar which he named 'Italia'. This was much revered at the time for its beautiful 'golden-vermilion' flowers, which were in the form of a cattleya orchid. *The Gardeners' Chronicle* of 14 December 1895 devoted a whole column to a detailed description of this plant, together with two illustrations.

'Atlanta', 'America', 'Austria', 'Burgundia' and 'Allemaniana' all followed. 'America' is still available. Not surprisingly, these were dubbed Italian or orchid-flowered cannas. At the Naples Flower Show in 1895, Dammann staged a 'gorgeous show' of them. They were much admired by the public – 'No words can express the beauty of the new varieties' – and were awarded the 'Diploma of Honour' by the judges. However, it seems that Sprenger did not succeed in his aim for increased hardiness. There are various references to displays of these new cannas under glass, which suggests that possibly they were not fully able to accept the rigours of a temperate summer. One French book shows a picture of an open-sided 'shelter' for cannas, which no doubt kept the worst of the rain from the flowers, while avoiding some of the problems of growing within a greenhouse.

CANNAS IN BRITAIN

By the 1890s, many of the French cannas had reached Britain. In his catalogue of 1890, James Veitch, the notable Exeter nurseryman, listed 13 cultivars, all with French or German names. By 1895, the list had grown to 33 and now included a sprinkling of English names. The 1896 catalogue has a resplendent print of canna flowers; even though it is in black and white, it shows the wide variety of flower markings and forms available then. The 1897 catalogue has a full-page illustration of 'Italia' and 'Austria', both available at 2s 6d each. By 1899, 73 cultivars were on offer and the catalogue had a full page devoted to an illustration of 'Grüss an Hamburg'. Amazingly, the price of 2s 6d each did not change during that period.

Kelways of Langport in Somerset, better known for irises, were offering 25 cannas in their 1893–94 list, of which six were their own. None of the names were registered, however, and they all seem to have been lost. Cannell and Sons of Swanley were growing cannas in large quantities: their 1897 catalogue lists 96 cultivars, including a number of Crozy's raising.

'Italia' was the novelty plant of 1897 and marked a key stage in the breeding programme.

The importance of cannas in horticulture during this period is further underlined by the fact that on 14 November 1893 George Paul, the celebrated nurseryman from Cheshunt, presented a paper about the genus to the Horticultural Club. This was subsequently printed in *The Gardeners' Chronicle* of 25 November 1893. It outlines the history of the genus, advances in hybridization, notable cultivars and cultural techniques. In particular, it is of interest to note the several references to flowering under glass in the winter. Alongside the article is an advertisement for Paul and Son but although roses, hollies and peonies are featured, there is only a one-word mention of cannas. Not the brash advertising link we might expect today!

THE SUBTROPICAL CRAZE

The frenzied hybridization of cannas coincided with the latter years of the bedding movement in England.

PLATE I

HERITAGE CANNAS

'Prince Charmant' (1892)

'Lafayette' (1925)

'Centenaire de Rozain-Boucharlat'
(early twentieth century)

'Shenandoah' (1894)

'Königin Charlotte' (1892)

'Sémaphore' (1895)

All flowers are shown at approximately half lifesize

'Oiseau de Feu' (1911)

'En Avant' (1914)

'Italia' (1893)

'Madame Angele
Martin' (1915)

'Wyoming' (1906)

'Florence Vaughan' (1893)

C. 'Warszewiczii' was another of the key parents in early canna breeding, adding dark foliage to the range.

With their bold foliage and exotic flowers, cannas were widely adopted as admirable subjects to include in summer-bedding schemes. Towards the end of the nineteenth century, garden fashions moved to encompass the style of bedding out that became known as 'subtropical'. It had been pioneered in the 1880s by Henry Cooke, a surgeon general in the army in India, who retired and returned home to Britain, where he proceeded to create an exotic garden. Many foliage and flowering plants from tropical climates, such as palms, cannas, coleus and bananas, were planted to create a lush, jungle-like atmosphere. Big displays of this style were also set up at Battersea Park in London by John Gibson, a renowned designer and gardener.

William Robinson was another advocate of the style. In his classic book *The Subtropical Garden*, he devoted 19 pages to descriptions of various cannas, which he regarded as important constituents of his gardens. 'A clump of cannas forms a beautiful group and contrasts splendidly with a fan-leaved palm or with such plants as Wigandias, Castor Oil Plants or some of the fine Aralias. The more distinctiveness there is in the plants used, the finer will be the tropical effect obtained and the greater the interest in the garden.'

However, Robinson particularly listed the older foliage cannas and made no reference to the newer types, as they were less suitable for creating the bold, exotic effect. Among those he mentioned, modern gardeners would recognize C. 'Edulis', C. *indica*, C. *iridiflora*, C. 'Limbata' and C. 'Warszewiczii', all of which are still available. Many of the others with amazing Latinized names, such as C. *Warszewiczioides-nobilis* and C. *rotundifolia-rubra-major*, are unknown today.

RHS TRIALS

The Royal Horticultural Society has held a number of trials of cannas. In 1893, at their gardens at Chiswick, some 45 cultivars were entered. Eleven received Awards of Merit and three were Highly Commended. Among the raisers were Veitch and Sons, Paul and Son, Lemoine and Vilmorin. From those selected, the only cultivar still grown is 'Königin Charlotte', which was granted an Award of Merit, although the RHS report of the time confusingly attributed it to Pfitzer and not Ernst.

We are not told whether the trial was outdoors or under glass, but editions of *The Gardeners' Chronicle* for July and September 1895 both carry articles recommending a visit to the RHS collection of cannas at Chiswick, 'where there are two houses in bloom'. This suggests that the trials were an ongoing feature.

A further trial was carried out at Chiswick in 1898. This time 71 cultivars were assessed; they were grown in large pots in an unheated greenhouse. One First Class Certificate was awarded to 'Admiral Courbet', submitted by Vilmorin, and 18 Awards of Merit were given to other submissions. Most of the names are unfamiliar, although among them are 'Florence Vaughan', 'Heinrich Seidel', 'Italia', 'Königin Charlotte', 'America' and 'Sémaphore', which are still available today. The Floral Committee commented that 'those of the 'Italia' group were conspicuous for their tall habit, handsome foliage and gorgeously coloured flowers, which were of shorter duration than the Crozy types.'

The last thorough trial of cannas was carried out at Wisley between 1906 and 1908. In the first two years, a collection of some 271 different stocks was amassed and initially assessed under glass. During 1908, some 200 of these were grown outside. From the original 271 cultivars, 220 distinct types were represented, suggesting that even then, there was confusion in naming, something that is a major headache some 90 years later. Although the trial classifies them as either orchid- or gladiolus-flowered, there is a comment that the differences between these two groups are now less distinct in some of the newer introductions. Again the only familiar names are 'Florence Vaughan', 'Italia', 'Königin Charlotte' and 'Sémaphore', with the addition of 'R. [Richard] Wallace', 'Shenandoah' and 'Wyoming'. From those planted outside in 1908, 16 were Highly Commended: all belonged to the gladiolus-flowered group but the only one known today is 'Richard Wallace'. The trial report listed all cultivars, dividing them up carefully into respective groups and colours.

CANNAS IN GERMANY

During the late nineteenth century, cannas also had a following in Germany. Wilhelm Pfitzer from Stuttgart started breeding in the 1890s. He is documented as having said that he did not think that his early introductions matched those of Crozy, although they did have a good dwarf habit. In 1893 he selected just seven or eight from among 400–500 planted-out seedlings. Pfitzer, who continued working until the 1950s, is particularly remembered for some of his later introductions, including 'Alberich', 'Gnom', 'Ingeborg', 'Perkeo', 'Puck', 'Richard Wallace' and 'Stadt Fellbach'. These are still widely grown today, as are some of those with colour epithets, such as 'Pfitzer's Cherry Red' and 'Pfitzer's Primrose Yellow'.

'Königin Charlotte' is a cultivar that appears consistently in lists from 1892 onwards. It was raised by G. Ernst, another German breeder working near Stuttgart. This is a short cultivar with medium-sized, red flowers broadly edged with yellow. It is enthusiastically described as the 'finest introduction to date' by Buckbee's of Illinois in their 1903 catalogue. It is still

The cover of this nineteenth century catalogue proudly displays the range of colours available in the early cannas.

widely grown today and is still regarded as an excellent cultivar, but it sometimes masquerades as 'Reine Charlotte' or 'Queen Charlotte', depending on the country of listing.

CANNAS IN THE USA

Cannas had also become popular in the USA. As part of the World's Columbian Exposition in Chicago in 1893, a massive planting was made, with over 76 beds, extending to over 300m (1000ft), sited in front of the main horticultural hall. The display was primarily planted with the new French (presumably Crozy) cultivars – an all-American canna, called 'Star of 91', was only present in a small bed and lacked 'staying power' and there was general agreement that 'Madame Crozy' was the best cultivar in the entire collection. Although the planting was said to have a 'spotty effect', it must, nevertheless, have been quite impres-

Hybrid number 1900, the subject of the name-that-canna competition in 1894. The prize was $100.

clear yellow with a dwarf habit, freedom of flowering and the ability to drop dying flowers cleanly. He also continued trying for the elusive white. Dingee and Conard introduced his 'Mont Blanc' in 1904, describing it as the 'nearest approach to a pure white. The flowers open creamy white and fade to a pure white.' By 1914 an 'Improved Mont Blanc' was being offered.

Sadly, 'Mont Blanc' (improved or original) is nothing more than a name today, as are Wintzer's other whites, 'Montano', 'Starlight' and 'Blanche Wintzer'. However, Wintzer must be credited with introducing nearly a hundred new cultivars before his death in 1923. 'Wyoming' is undoubtedly the best known of his creations and probably still one of the most widely grown cannas. 'The President', 'City of Portland' and 'Wintzer's Colossal' are also still available worldwide. Although, by modern standards, their huge stature may not always be acceptable, their vigour and disease-resistance are still good enough to enable them to hold their own among more recent introductions.

At roughly the same time as M. Sprenger embarked on his breeding programme in Italy, which resulted in the orchid-flowered cannas, Luther Burbank of California was carrying out similar crosses. We know of two of his successes, 'Tarrytown', whose description sounds remarkably like 'Italia', and 'Burbank', which he produced in 1897. If he bred others, their names seem to have been lost with the passing of time.

Name that canna

New canna cultivars attracted considerable interest at the end of the nineteenth century and the naming of new cultivars was, therefore, quite critical. In the April 1894 edition of their in-house magazine, *Success with Flowers*, Dingee and Conard announced a competition to name their new hybrid 'Number 1900', described as the 'grandest and most beautiful canna ever grown'. The prize was a princely $100.

A final reminder of the competition appeared in the August edition of *Success with Flowers*, but annoyingly, the subsequent editions of the magazine have yet to be located, so we may never know the name of this 'grandest canna'.

SEED

Named cultivars must be propagated by division. However, in the late nineteenth century, seed was still

sive. There seems to be a competitive element within the exhibits as there is reference to other displays by New York and Pennsylvania, whose plantings were considered to be better, although not so extensive.

One of the major contributors to the American canna heritage is a Frenchman named Antoine Wintzer (some references refer to Leon Wintzer) who was employed by the Dingee and Conard Company of West Grove, Pennsylvania. In 1894, he teamed up with Dr Van Fleet of the US Department of Agriculture, who had produced the first 'near-white' canna, 'Alsace', and the first bright red, 'Flamingo'.

They worked together for a while; Van Fleet then went back to rose breeding and Wintzer continued with cannas. His next objective was a pure yellow, with which his first great success was 'Buttercup', a considered as an alternative way of raising plants and seed of the various species was offered, as well as mixtures. Arthur Henderson's seed catalogue of 1871 listed 21 different types, including such names as 'Annei, Coccinea, Flaccida, Musaefolia and Zebrina', all at between 4d and 6d per packet. Later on, mixtures of bedding type cannas were offered. However, it is doubtful that the 'New Crozy' canna seed offered at 10 cents a packet by Parks of Pennsylvania in 1894 had ever been near Lyons!

BOOKS ON CANNAS

The popularity of cannas at the turn of the nineteenth century is revealed by the number of books written on the subject. *The Canna and How to Grow It* by B. C. Ravenscroft was published in 1903 in English. Advice on cultivation, display and hybridization is given, along with detailed lists of cultivars. The first is 'A list of forty of the best gladiolus flowered varieties', recommended for culture in pots and for show purposes, followed by 'A list of half-a-dozen fine dwarf cannas', for bedding. Then there is 'One hundred good older or standard varieties' for bedding or pot culture and, finally, a further 28, including the famed 'Italia', listed as 'Orchid flowering varieties'. The year before, Paul Pallary had produced *Le Canna et Ses Variétés. Culture, Hybridation et Emplois en France et Algerie Horticoles*. These were followed in 1909 by a German book, *Das Geschlecht der Canna* by Árpád Mühle.

CANNAS IN AUSTRALIA

Between the two world wars, many new varieties were produced by an Australian breeder called Cole, who was working near Albury, New South Wales around 1930. 'Rosemond Coles', which it seems likely that Cole raised, is a well-known and widely grown yellow and red bicoloured cultivar but otherwise very few of his splendid introductions are frequently cultivated, although they are still available in Australia and New Zealand and are well worth growing.

It is thought that Cole named his new creations after ancestors listed in his family bible. 'King Cole' is believed to have been named after the family patriarch King Khole, a German who lived in the Colewood, near Woodchurch, Kent, England. 'Cornelius Cole' is said to be named after the son of a minister in the western district of Victoria, who died,

at the age of nine months, in the 1800s. These are intriguing stories, but little can be verified and the real Cole has been elusive, even to the extent of his unknown first name.

CANNAS IN INDIA

Cannas have been widely grown in India at various times, but as in so many places, their popularity has waxed and waned. The following extract by Kathleen Murray, from *The Virago Book of Women Gardeners* (1913), delightfully illustrates one such fall from favour:

'Fashions in flowers are almost as evanescent as fashions in millinery. It is not long since canna was all the rage; every garden I know was full of it and people who had never gardened before became pronounced bores on the subject of canna, which appeals to the beginner as being a nice easy plant to grow. You planted it in any corner of your garden, the newer the soil the better, and no sooner had you planted it than – hey presto! It flowered gorgeously, sending up a quantity of suckers for the furtherance of its species. In fact, canna seemed almost too good to be true.

It was barely a year before a doubt crept in. The canna groups had a way of getting untidy, and the mali forgot to cut down the stems that had flowered. In time it dawned on us that canna was a greedy and ungrateful creature, an insatiable feeder, a thirsty drinker. It speedily exhausted the soil and it clamoured for more. We discovered that canna loved change, and must be transplanted every three months or so, and gradually we fell out of love with it. It was still gorgeous, but so easily propagated that every garden blazed with it; we wearied of its magnificence. And so canna fell into its proper place. It serves to fill a space, and it flowers often when there is little else in the garden, but it is in no sense to be relied, and it is deceptive in that it requires more care than it professes to.

Cosmos is now the fashion, and its starlike blossoms are dainty and easy to arrange.'

However, despite such dismissal, Agnes Harler's *The Garden in the Plains*, printed by the Diocesan Press, Madras in 1941, has a section on cannas. They obviously hadn't been totally abandoned! There is a short list of cultivars grown in India; these mostly have English names and include cultivars such as 'The President', 'Statue of Liberty', 'Copper Giant' and 'Black Knight' (the earliest reference I can find to this name). A much more recent Indian list of 1982 still includes a number of these older cultivars, together with well-known names, such as 'Cleopatra', 'City of Portland' and 'King Humbert', suggesting an ongoing western influence in Indian gardening.

The name of S. Percy Lancaster is linked with cannas in India as was that of his father, Percy Joseph Lancaster, who worked on cannas between 1889 and 1904 at the Royal Agri-Horticultural Society in Alipore, Calcutta, and produced many hybrids including one named after himself. 'Percy Lancaster' is described as being of medium stature with yellow flowers, heavily spotted with red. A black and white photograph in the little book *The Canna*, published by the Indian Council of Research, shows an attractive flower with markings similar to 'Florence Vaughan' or 'Italia'. The most thorough scientific study of cannas, 'Evolution of Cultivated Cannas' by T. N. Khoshoo and I. Guha, was published in *Glimpses in Plant Research*, an Indian, English-language publication, in 1976 (see also p.57).

THE FALL FROM FASHION

Despite their initial good start at the turn of the century, sometime in the first half of the twentieth century cannas became unpopular in Britain. This was probably linked with the demise of the formal bedding system that gave way to the more relaxed garden features, such as the herbaceous border, championed by well-known names, such as William Robinson and Gertrude Jekyll. (Jekyll did, however, use cannas in her schemes, although she often used vague references such as 'yellow canna', rather than a cultivar name.) The two world wars were also responsible for the downfall of the big private estates with their armies of gardeners and ranks of greenhouses. One can imagine that plants as demanding of time and heat as cannas would have been some of the first to be abandoned.

The powerful effect of fashion trends should not be ignored. After so many years of popularity, it is likely that gardeners simply tired of cannas and garden writers either ignored them or deprecated them, resulting in their loss of vogue. Such trends have an alarming effect on the conservation of tender plants such as these. Whereas specimens of hardy plants, especially trees and shrubs, would remain in neglected gardens, plants that require nurturing, such as cannas, are almost immediately lost. Although a few of the better and tougher types remained in some gardens, by far the majority of those hundreds of cultivars that were grown at the end of the nineteenth century were lost in Britain and many other temperate areas.

By 1991, when I started collecting cannas, there were probably only 18 cultivars and species available from nurseries in Britain. In warmer climates, cannas retained some of their popularity because of their ability to flower for long periods and it is from these countries – Australia, India and New Zealand and the southern states of the USA – that some of the old cultivars are being rediscovered. No doubt many others remain, neglected and not lost but lacking their identity.

Some gardeners have always recognized the value of cannas. It is interesting to read a piece entitled 'The Neglected Canna', penned in 1957 by that doyen of gardening writers, Christopher Lloyd. In a full-page article in *The Gardeners' Chronicle*, he extols their virtues, lists his choice of cultivars and describes their cultivation. He starts off by commenting 'how seldom one sees cannas in English gardens nowadays! even in London!' He bemoans the fact that there are no pink cultivars available in Britain and drools over the description of a white canna that had been 'sighted' in Ghana.

CANNA STUDIES

There seems to have been little detailed study of cannas in the twentieth century and, as a minor ornamental, virtually no scientific research. However, in 1982 a trial was carried out in Florida. This took place at the Agricultural Research and Education Center of the University of Florida. Fifty-two cultivars were planted in field conditions and assessed for various characteristics. The results of this trial, although fascinating, can only be regarded as relevant in relationship to climates similar to Florida. Even some of the broader results, such as height, can be misleading. For example, 'Wyoming' is regarded as a dwarf under Florida conditions as it is regularly decimated by canna leaf-roller caterpillar. This pest is unknown in Britain, where 'Wyoming' regularly tops 1.8m (6ft). Although the rate of seed set is recorded, giving an indication of the ongoing productivity, there is no record of those cultivars that drop their dead flowers and are, therefore, self-cleaning. While the trial notes make interesting reading, the results should be very carefully interpreted by those growing cannas under temperate conditions.

'QUEEN OF THE CANNAS'
No account of canna growing should omit to mention Mrs Rosalind Sarver, known by many as the 'Queen of the Cannas', who ran a commercial nursery in San Marcos, California for nearly 50 years. Although she grew other plants, over 2 hectares (5 acres) of land were devoted to canna production. Her 1978 list shows an appreciation of the traditional types, including The Grand Opera Series, 'President' and 'Lucifer', as well as modern types, such as 'Lippo' and 'Rosever' (an abbreviation of her own name perhaps), which she notes as 'new'. As late as 1995, she was corresponding with fellow growers and hybridists regarding new introductions. Her 1997–98 catalogue explains that under the warm Californian climate, cannas are kept growing all the year so that fresh rootstocks are dug for each order. Mrs Sarver was still active in her nursery when she died, aged 92, in 1998. The obituaries speak glowingly of a life-long devotion to cannas.

THE RENAISSANCE
The last decade of the twentieth century and beginning of the twenty-first has seen a considerable revival of interest in the canna in many parts of the world. In Britain, this has coincided with a growth in interest in exotic-looking plants, very much a renaissance of the subtropical style of gardening promoted by William Robinson at the end of the nineteenth century. A series of warm summers and mild winters has encouraged gardeners to be more adventurous in planting species on the borderline of hardiness, generally all with exotic-looking foliage and flowers. Bananas, tree ferns, cordylines and yuccas, to name just a few, have been planted in their thousands, sometimes with amazing results. subtropical gardens, such as that created by Will Giles in Norwich, have met with great success and Christopher Lloyd's dramatic replanting of the traditional rose garden at his family home of Great Dixter, while initially greeted with shock and horror, is now widely acclaimed. In all these schemes, cannas are an essential ingredient.

2

BOTANY

Cannas belong to the plant family Cannaceae, which contains only one genus, *Canna* itself. The family belongs to the plant order Zingiberales, which means that it is loosely related to some other tropical families such as Musaceae, Zingiberaceae, Heliconiaceae, Costaceae, Marantaceae, Lowiaceae and Strelitziaceae. As well as many exotic ornamentals, the familiar commercial fruiting banana is within the family Musaceae. Among the huge family of Zingiberaceae, there are many grown as medicinal herbs or spices, such as ginger, as well as exotic cut flowers and garden plants. Marantaceae includes ornamentals such as the prayer plant (*Maranta*) and a species grown for a commercial starch. The other families, although less well known, include many beautiful ornamental plants, grown worldwide, of which *Strelitzia*, the bird-of-paradise, is probably the most familiar.

The original habitat of cannas is tropical areas of South America, with one species coming from Florida. They are, however, abundantly naturalized throughout the tropics and subtropics. The proliferation of primary hybrids in these situations has led to considerable confusion regarding the naming of all cannas and in particular the wild species.

EDIBLE CANNA

A canna grower once commented, on dividing some rather vigorous cannas, that he wished his King Edwards (the potato cultivar) were as productive! In fact, his comment was not far off the mark, as at least one form of canna is edible and has been grown in

South America for over 5,000 years. This species is usually known as C. 'Edulis', although it is, in fact, a form of C. *indica*. Its rootstocks are a unique source of easily digested starch, the grains of which are 100 times the size of aroid starch. It should not, however, be confused with refined arrowroot, which is produced from a species of *Maranta*.

As a commercial crop, C. 'Edulis' is known as purple arrowroot, Queensland arrowroot, *tous-les-mois* or *achira*. The edible part is the thick, fleshy rhizome, which develops near the soil surface. There are both white- and purple-skinned types, giving rise to one of the commonly used names. The foliage is generally green, although the purple-skinned types usually have purple stems, leaf ribs and leaf margins. Flowers are irrelevant to the crop, but are either orange or red. It is still produced as a food crop in South America, especially Peru and Columbia, where it is seldom eaten raw but often baked. In Australia, it is produced on an intensive scale for industrial starch and, in Vietnam and parts of East Asia, it is grown and highly valued as a source of flour for noodle production.

This crop is most successful in moist soils and where temperatures are between 25°C (77°F) and 28°C (82°F). It is, however, an adaptable plant and grows well at altitudes as high as 2,600m (8,500ft) or more. It also does well where temperatures are lower and other starchy crops, such as cassava, are less productive. It is not, however, successful where drought is likely. Taking about eight months to mature from planting to harvest, the plant yields range from 12 to 25 tonnes (12–24½ tons) per hectare (2½ acres). The largest rhizomes may be up to 60cm (24in) long and some may contain up to 25 per cent starch.

'Dondo' is one of a number of very pale-flowered cannas sometimes referred to as 'whites'.

C. 'Edulis' was introduced to Britain as an ornamental in 1820. Here plants grow to as much as 3m (10ft) and have leaves as long as 60cm (24in).

WHAT ARE CANNAS?

Cannas are erect herbaceous perennials that will grow continuously when climatic conditions are suitable. When warmth, light and moisture is the same as they would receive in their native environment, there is a continuous process whereby plants produce shoots that flower, set seed and die down, by which time new shoots have appeared to take their place. Under such conditions, the canna would normally only go dormant if there is insufficient moisture to enable growth to proceed. Then the fleshy rhizomes enable the plant to survive until fresh water supplies stimulate re-growth. It is this dormancy mechanism that allows cannas to be grown in colder countries, where they go dormant for the cold winter months.

RHIZOMES

The rhizome, although produced underground and looking like a root, is actually a thick, fleshy, horizontal, stem-like structure. It is from this that the fibrous roots are produced and the buds for shoot growth. The rhizome sits on or near the surface of the soil. Its size and shape varies considerably, from the huge fleshy structure of C. 'Edulis', to the smaller ones of C. indica

Canna rhizomes are actually swollen horizontal stems that produce roots and buds for shoot growth.

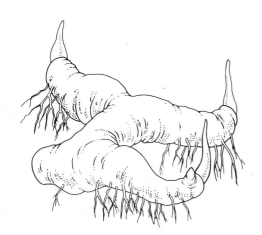

or the long, wiry types found on C. glauca and its derivatives. Some, such as C. 'Musifolia', produce very short rhizomes, not much more than a swollen base to the flowering stem. These either have to be stored very carefully to prevent them from shrivelling away, or, ideally, have to be kept growing through the winter under greenhouse conditions. I have seen at least one place where canna rhizomes are described as being either like tubers (plump and sizeable) or like stolons (thin and wiry). Such descriptions may be practically helpful, but should not be taken too literally as all cannas are rhizomatous.

Another important aspect of the rhizome is the number of shoots it is able to produce. A good-quality canna rhizome may be sold as a 'three-eye root', which means that there are three dormant buds, each of which should be able to produce a shoot. A study in India in 1970 compared the 'tillering' ability of several cultivars with the wild species. In general, wild species cannas produce more tillers than cultivars and diploids produce more than triploids. Inevitably those cultivars that have a high tillering rate are easily propagated. It is not surprising, therefore, that cultivars which produce many shoots, and subsequently many rhizomes, such as 'Perkeo', 'Strasbourg' and 'Robert Kemp', are very widely obtainable. Sadly, some less scrupulous nurserymen will substitute these types, which are always available, for the more desirable short-supply cultivars.

STEMS AND LEAVES

The stems are rigid and each shoot is finite, generally producing between six and nine leaves before flowering commences. The leaves are large, spirally arranged around the stem and generally broadly elliptical or oblong. There is a prominent midrib, which is sometimes coloured differently from the leaf blade. The leaves are pinnately veined (see p.25) and the short petiole (stalk) sheaves the stem. The leaf margin is entire, although sometimes undulate (wavy). The apex is described as acute or short acuminate, which simply means that it is pointed, and sometimes twisted. Each new leaf appears, rolled up, at the top of the stem as it grows. They unfurl gradually until they sometimes begin to hang because of their own weight. The leaves of triploids are thicker than those of diploids. In some species, such as C. glauca, the leaf is narrow and glau-

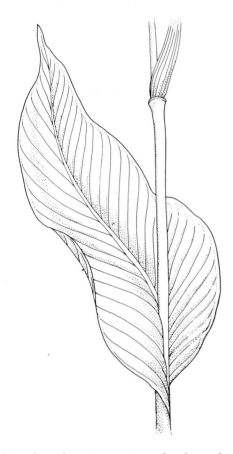

Canna leaves have pinnate veins and are borne alternately on the stem.

A racemose inflorescence, the most common flower formation.

cous. In some measure, these characteristics have been transferred to some of the hybrids we now grow, particularly the water cannas (p.38), which are closely related to C. *glauca*.

FLOWERS AND FRUIT

The flower spike is generally a racemose inflorescence, meaning that it flowers from the base upwards to the tip of the spike. Most wild species have a simple unbranched raceme with relatively few flowers. The exceptions to this are C. *paniculata* and C. *iridiflora*, both of which have branched racemes, called panicles; these are dense inflorescences with numerous flowers. Cultivars have panicles. The number of branches in an inflorescence may vary from one to eight. Many-branched types are preferred because of the continuity of flowering and quantity of bloom provided. These

C. *iridiflora* bears flowers in a panicle.

PLATE II

SMALL-FLOWERED AND SPECIES CANNAS

'Taney' (water canna)

C. *indica*

C. *iridiflora*
'Ehemanii'

'Edulis'

'Intrigue'

'Warszewiczii'

'Heliconifolia'

'Robert Kemp'

'Erebus'
(water canna)

'Ra' (water canna)

'Isis'

C. glauca

All flowers are shown at approximately lifesize

3

CULTIVATION

Canna rhizomes can be purchased in the spring. In garden centres and catalogues, they are sometimes called tubers or even bulbs, neither of which is botanically correct. When buying the rhizomes, make sure that they are plump, not shrivelled: ideally, the cannas will have been dug and dispatched before they have had a chance to become dormant and desiccated, but shops and garden centres are often too warm and dry for the rhizomes, which may result in them becoming dehydrated. Although it is sometimes possible to revive such purchases, they are slow to develop and may refuse to grow at all.

Buying by mail order can also be a little uncertain, although most reputable suppliers will respond to a genuine complaint. As with any other purchase, you need to accept the risks when buying cheap bargain packs. Some companies may specify the number of 'eyes'; at least one prominent supplier in the USA offers '3–5 eye bulbs', and guarantees that they will all grow.

If any delay is likely before potting the rhizomes, they should be kept in a cool, frost-free place and care taken that they do not dry out. Packing into a tray of damp peat or compost to avoid desiccation is a wise precaution for any extended delay. This technique can also be used to re-hydrate dry rhizomes before properly planting.

Although it is possible to plant dormant cannas directly into the ground outside, many gardeners in temperate areas will find it beneficial to start them in a greenhouse or polytunnel. Older textbooks often suggest that they should be started in high temperatures very early in the year. Not only is this expensive and impractical for most gardeners, but it is generally unnecessary as cannas grow fast and a good--sized plant can be produced and start to flower in midsummer, by planting as late as mid-spring with only minimal extra heat. See also Propagation, pp.46–53.

SITE

As they come from tropical and subtropical regions of the world, it is not surprising that cannas need a warm, sunny site to grow and thrive. A position against a south- or west-facing wall is ideal as this will benefit from the additional heat radiated from the wall, giving earlier flowering and, if the clumps are to be left in the ground, some winter protection. However, such cosseting is not essential and I have rarely seen cannas blown over in the wind, so an open site is not a problem.

Cannas will survive in a shady site but they are unlikely to grow as profusely and the darker-leaved cultivars are likely to lose their colour, so it is not generally recommended. The exception to this is in the hotter states of the USA and warmer parts of Europe, where there are constant high temperatures and long hours of sunshine during the summer months. Under these conditions, a site that will get shade for up to 50 per cent of the day may be advantageous as the flowers will last longer.

SOIL PREPARATION

However cannas are grown, whether as a seasonal display, replanting each year, or as a permanent feature, the initial border cultivation is similar. Ideally

'Champigny' is ideal for growing in a container. It is seen here with *Nemesia* 'Confetti', petunias and a bronze cordyline.

soil preparation should start well in advance, the previous autumn or winter, and should begin with deep digging. Although the technique of double digging is unfashionable, such deep cultivation can only be beneficial for plants such as cannas. Generally, turning the soil with a rotary cultivator does not break it up to an adequate depth and may actually cause a 'pan', which will impede drainage.

A heavy dressing of garden compost, manure or other organic matter should be incorporated at the cultivation stage. The best cannas I ever grew were on the site of an old barn, where the soil was black from years of accumulated droppings and rotted straw. Organic matter is important in improving the structure of all types of soil. It helps to encourage good crumb structure and both aids the retention of water in sandy soils and allows the penetration of air into heavy clay soils. It will also provide some nutrients, especially trace elements. One grower has suggested that it may also be effective in raising the soil temperature as the organic matter decays. Soils high in organic matter will also be darker and therefore absorb more radiant heat. On this basis, organic matter is of particular importance in cooler climates such as Britain. After cultivation, the soil surface should be left rough over the winter to weather naturally.

Cannas prefer to grow at about pH6.5, which is just slightly on the acid side of neutral. Lime should be applied only if a pH test shows significant soil acidity, as they do not like alkaline soils. When it is necessary to apply lime, this should be done in the autumn to allow the pH changes to take place over the winter months.

A couple of weeks before planting, the soil should be raked and trodden down to a level and crumbly surface. If there are any weeds, it is beneficial to hoe them off at this point. Perennial weeds can be controlled by a translocated herbicide such as Glyphosate, which is not held by the soil so is quite safe to use at this stage. A fine tilth is not needed as the clumps for planting are quite large and will usually be planted with a spade. A balanced general-purpose fertilizer should be applied and raked in at the same time. Although the recommended rates should not be exceeded, cannas do like a very rich soil, so where the manufacturer recommends a graded rate of application, the higher rate can be used. Cannas appreciate

an open, loose soil, so every effort should be made to avoid compacting it by over-working it or cultivating it when wet.

PLANTING OUT

Canna plants should not be planted out into the garden until all danger of frost is past, generally late spring and early summer. If conditions are cool or soil temperature is likely to be cold, there is no advantage to be gained from rushing the planting. Quite late plantings seem to catch up if conditions are right, whereas early plantings into a cold, wet soil seem to sulk.

Planting distance varies with different types. However, virtually all cannas are greedy and like plenty of space, so it is wise to be generous. The smallest dwarfs could be spaced about 45cm (18in) apart, most medium or standard cultivars at 60cm (2ft), with the spacing increasing to about 90cm (3ft) for the most vigorous tall cultivars. Allocated space is also affected by whether the cannas are to be grown on their own or interplanted with other lower-growing plants as a groundcover. Where several plants of the same cultivar are used to make a group with a big impact, closer spacing, down to as little as 30cm (1ft), is appropriate within the group, allowing more room between groups or adjacent plants. Where there are many different cultivars planted together, close spacing can be a problem in the autumn, when clumps will have grown into each other and rhizomes can become muddled.

After planting, unless rain is imminent, the plants should be well watered in. As a precaution, it is wise to scatter slug pellets around the whole area. At every stage, it is essential to make sure that named cultivars retain their labels and the planting stage is one occasion when they can easily be lost. I have also seen jackdaws remove plant labels, so where there is a collection of cultivars whose names are important, a sketch of locations can be a useful insurance.

DIRECT PLANTING

For those that do not have a greenhouse or conservatory in which to start their plants, canna rhizomes may be planted directly into the open soil. In temperate climates, this is not an ideal technique: in cool summers growth may be slow and the plants may fail to flower. However, if you wish to try this, do not plant the dormant rhizomes until late spring. As well as the preparation described above, a little sharp sand or grit should be put in the planting hole before placing the rhizome, which should be planted about 10cm (4in) deep. On cold nights, the emerging shoots must be protected from frost with some sort of temporary cover such as horticultural fleece.

AFTERCARE

If the season is dry, additional watering is essential as cannas will not grow and thrive in dry conditions. Almost any type of garden sprinkler that will apply water evenly can be used, although the overhead types may become a problem later in the season, when flowering commences, as the petals will be damaged by the water. Low-level irrigation, such as lay-flat tubing that directs the water out at the base of the plants, is preferable. In order to maximize the value of watering, a mulch of organic matter is a sensible addition. Garden compost, leaf mould, coir or bark are all possibilities and should be spread between 5 to 7.5cm (2–3in) thick. Such a luxury is not wasted as it merely forms part of the autumn dressing when the bed is dug the next time.

Under most conditions, growth will be rapid and flowering usually starts in midsummer, although a cold season can delay this by a few weeks. Cannas are greedy feeders so a mid-season dressing with a general fertilizer helps to promote a good display. This should be applied carefully around each plant, avoiding the foliage, and gently hoed in to the surface; if conditions are dry, it should be irrigated in. Apart from keeping them weed-free and a watch for pests and diseases, little other attention is needed.

Flowering will continue into the autumn until the first frosts. The meticulous grower may wish to deadhead the plants as the old flowers fade and this should be done with care. Each individual flower lasts only a few days and after its peak will either fall to the ground or shrivel up and look untidy. It is the latter blooms that need to be removed, avoiding damage to the surrounding unopened buds. Care should always be taken to avoid being stung, as bees and wasps frequently visit the flowers and can be hidden among the crumpled petals. As flowering proceeds, it eventually becomes apparent that the flower spike has no more buds. At this stage, it can be removed with secateurs or a sharp knife but only down to the next side shoot, where a secondary flower spike will appear. Usually most cannas will produce two, three or four spikes, getting increasingly smaller until the whole stem is spent and must be removed from the base. Under most temperate garden conditions, this is not achieved until the end of the season.

OVERWINTERING

As it is a tender perennial, the canna's top growth will not withstand any frost. Under tropical conditions, cannas normally continue to grow throughout the year and dormancy is not part of the normal cycle. However, in climates where frost occurs, the life cycle is modified and the plant becomes dormant over the winter months. Amazingly, it adapts to this very well. However, it must be remembered that cannas have a rhizome, not a bulb, and whereas bulbs are able to dry out completely and remain viable, the canna rhizome will easily die if allowed to become too dry.

As soon as temperatures drop below freezing, the top growth will brown and instantly die. If the roots freeze, they will also die. For this reason, under temperate conditions, provision must be made to protect the roots over winter. This normally means that some time in mid- to late autumn, they must be lifted and taken to a frost-free store. If the autumn display is good, there is no reason why the plants cannot be left in the ground for the display to continue until the first frost blackens the foliage. The only drawback with this is that by late autumn the soil can be quite wet, making the lifting process muddy and laborious. Also there is always the risk that the first frost, when late in the year, may be a hard one and the soil might freeze, which could damage the roots and make them difficult or impossible to lift.

Where there are different cultivars, it is most important to ensure that each plant is clearly labelled before lifting. Once dormant, very few cannas can be identified from their rhizomes. A plastic label of the type with a hole in it is the most suitable for this job, and the name must be clearly printed with indelible ink. The simplest technique for labelling is to cut down the plants to leave about 15cm (6in) of stem, onto which the label can be tied with thin wire or polypropylene string. It should be tied tightly as the stems will shrivel over the winter, allowing the knot to loosen. Where

PLATE III

CANNA LEAVES

'Grande' (green),
'Pink Sunburst' (striped)

'Stuttgart'

'Durban'
(orange form)

'Italia'

All leaves are shown at approximately one third lifesize

'Lucifer'

'Mystique'

C. glauca

'Australia'

'Pretoria'

there are several clumps of the same cultivar, storing them together in boxes, with each box labelled, may be easier.

The cutting-down process is quite straightforward and secateurs may be used for most cannas, although some of the more vigorous ones may have stems too large for cutting with secateurs, in which case a small saw may need to be used. The waste from cannas is lush and will compost quite easily. As it is bulky it is best chopped up or, ideally, shredded before composting and then it rots easily.

DIGGING UP

After removing the top growth, the roots should be dug up carefully, making sure to avoid damaging any of the rhizomes as this can encourage rotting overwinter. Particular care should be taken when lifting plants of C. glauca, the related water cannas and 'Stuttgart', all of which have long, fragile rhizomes. Not only do these break easily, but they are inclined to travel some distance and all parts need to be carefully retrieved from neighbouring plants to avoid muddling. Excess soil can be shaken off, although many growers find that some soil left around the roots helps to maintain them in a stable condition until the spring.

The lifted roots must be stored in a cool but frost-free environment. Under commercial conditions cannas are stored in bulky containers with slatted sides for air circulation and the temperature is controlled to ensure that the plants neither grow nor deteriorate over the winter. Under domestic conditions, storage might be in a frost-free garage, cellar, shed or attic. Wherever, it should be no higher than 10°C (50°F) and must never drop below freezing. Many growers also have success with storing dormant cannas under the benches of a cool greenhouse. In this case, a small heater with a thermostat set a few degrees above freezing should be used.

Commercial growers also emphasize the importance of humidity during storage. Ideally, the humidity would be around 30–50 per cent, but this is only critical if the roots have been washed of all soil and are bare. Care must be taken to ensure that humidity does not encourage early growth or fungal disorders. When growing a range of cannas, one soon observes that there are distinct differences in the rhizomes, some being very fat and round, while others, such as C. glau-

ca, are thin and stringy. Inevitably, the thinner ones are those that are more prone to desiccation and it is important that these are kept moist in the winter. When they are stored under greenhouse benches, a small amount of drip from above may actually be beneficial, preventing the roots from shrivelling.

In store, the rhizomes should be stacked close together, in trays or on shelves, with peat, bark or old potting compost around the roots to prevent desiccation. If the roots were dry when lifted, this media should be damp when used. If, however, the clumps were wet when lifted, dry peat or bark can be used to absorb some of the excess moisture. It is worth giving a dusting of fungicide (such as sulphur, captan, maneb or zineb) at this stage as a precaution against fungal infection, which may set into any small cuts or damaged rhizomes. The remainder of the stem can sometimes decay with various moulds, which then infect the rhizomes, and sulphur will deter this.

Over the winter months, there is very little to do, although the rhizomes should be inspected at regular intervals. The most important point to remember is that they must never dry out completely nor must they become too wet. This means careful monitoring and trying to keep a uniform state of moisture. There are no easy guidelines but generally, if the rhizomes and surrounding media start to feel very dry, a light sprinkling of water should be applied. In this instance, it is wisest to be cautious and err on the side of a light watering, applying more later if needed.

Plants in pots store very easily but those grown in loamless composts must be watched carefully as they dry out more quickly and can easily become totally desiccated. For some reason, pot-bound plants in smaller pots seem to survive better than plants in large pots or tubs. Sometimes vigorous cannas in pots send out strong rhizomes which 'dive' to the bottom of the pots. These easily die over winter.

Towards the end of the winter, it is important to increase the moisture content slightly to ensure that the rhizomes are fully turgid before dividing and potting. If shoots start to emerge, then potting and division should take place before they become etiolated and weak. Taking plants out of store is another time when labels can easily be separated from their plants: stems may have shrivelled and string may have slipped; also, if soil has dried, clumps may easily fall apart so care must be taken to keep each plant carefully with its label.

ALTERNATIVE STORAGE METHOD

One amateur grower successfully stores his cannas in a modified 'clamp', a traditional storage method for potatoes and root vegetables. Most of his plants are pot grown but the technique could also be used for lifted clumps. At the end of the summer he cuts the plants down and tips them out of their pots. The rootballs are packed tight together in a large block on the floor of his greenhouse. The gaps are filled with dry peat and the whole area left until the peat has absorbed any excess moisture from the rootballs. The block is then covered with several layers of horticultural bubble insulation, well tucked in at the edges. Every three weeks, the insulation is removed to ventilate the block. If there are any signs of mould, a copper-based fungicide is used. Mouse bait is also used! In very cold conditions additional polystyrene insulation is used, but no heat.

OVERWINTERING OUTSIDE

Many gardeners find the process of lifting and storing cannas tedious and time consuming. Fortunately, the rhizomes are on the borderline of hardiness and in milder areas it is possible to leave them in the ground with reasonable success. This alternative does, however, have an element of a gamble. Although it may be successful for a number of mild winters, eventually there is likely to be a cold winter when such outdoor stocks will be lost.

If you are anticipating planting cannas in this semi-permanent way, the initial choice and preparation of site is most important. A well-drained soil and a warm location is essential. Some authorities suggest that cannas that have been less heavily fed may be more able to withstand harsh winter conditions. It is, therefore, recommended that the second fertilizer dressing is omitted. At the end of the season, after the first frost, the plants should be cut back in the normal way and each clump very carefully labelled. Again, it may be worth making a sketch plan showing the locations of different varieties as labels can be removed by birds over the winter or shattered by frost.

Each clump is then deeply covered with a generous layer of insulating mulch. This should be light and open, not too wet and stodgy. Partially composted leaves, straw, bracken or rough garden compost are ideal, while farmyard manure is too heavy and wet: the aim is to create a layer of insulation, rather than feed or cap the soil; air spaces are essential. The layer should be at least 15cm (6in) deep and extend over the whole anticipated area of the roots. With a whole bed of cannas, it is most practical to mulch the entire soil surface.

Well before growth is likely in early spring, slug pellets should be used as the mulch provides ideal shelter for slugs and snails, and damage is quite likely. By spring, the mulch will usually have been partially decomposed and its depth reduced so there should be no problem with the emergence of the new shoots. In fact the remaining mulch will help to protect those young shoots if there are any late frosts.

Cannas grown in this way generally start to flower a week or so later than those grown by lifting and starting under glass but are usually equally successful by the end of the season. The planting should never be considered as permanent as the cannas will need dividing every three to five years, just like any other herbaceous perennial. Without this, the clumps become congested, growth weak and flowering poor. More research needs to be done on which cultivars are the most successful for growing in this way.

CONSERVATORY CULTIVATION

Cannas will provide a long-lasting display for conservatories, atria and greenhouses. Even when not in flower, their striking foliage is a valuable asset. In such situations, they can be grown in large pots or tubs or they can be planted out in border soil where this is available.

Under conservatory conditions, flowering will start earlier and continue later into the autumn. Some of the larger types, such as C. 'Musifolia', stand a greater chance of achieving their full potential when they are protected in this way. Where the structure is heated to 10°C (50°F) or higher, growth and flowering will continue throughout the winter months. Although flowering is not as generous as in the summer, even just a touch of tropical colour is always welcome in the winter.

All cultivars can be grown under glass, but it is more valuable for some than others. Those that used to be

Most cannas will perform to perfection under greenhouse conditions. 'Shenandoah' is shown here.

categorized as orchid-flowered, such as 'Florence Vaughan', are particularly successful. Their fragile flowers are often spoiled by the weather outside and the protection of glass will allow them to flaunt their delicate beauty to the greatest advantage. Coming from very hot climates, cannas do not normally need any shading under glass in the summer and I have rarely seen sun scorch where other conditions are satisfactory: if, however, the high temperatures and bright sunlight are coupled with water shortage, scorch may result. Light shading has an advantage in that it seems to make the individual flowers last a little longer and, in the case of a conservatory, makes the whole environment a more pleasant one in which to work or relax. Adjustable blinds are ideal and enable the structure to be shaded at the hottest periods of the day or year without restricting light at other times.

POTS INDOORS

When using containers of any sort for this sort of cultivation, the emphasis should be on selecting ones with a generous capacity – unlike many plants, cannas perform best when they have ample root run. By the time they have become pot-bound, their vigour will have declined and so will their flowering. Any good potting medium can be used, either loam-based, such as John Innes No 3, or a loamless equivalent. When a loamless compost is used, it is especially important to add a slow-release fertilizer to ensure a steady release of nutrients. A coarse compost, if available, is preferable to the fine grades often offered for general use.

Where good, well-rotted garden compost or farmyard manure is available, a layer of this in the bottom of large pots can be quite beneficial. It provides good drainage and a source of additional nutrients when roots reach the base of the pots, and it is considerably cheaper than filling the whole pot with bought compost. However, a proprietary well-balanced potting compost should always be used for the bulk of the rooting zone.

Under glass, cannas need an enormous amount of water and at the peak of summer, large plants in full growth may need to be top-watered twice a day. Alternatively, they can be stood in shallow saucers of water keeping the roots constantly moist. A simple way of achieving this with large pots is to stand them in half-filled plastic washing-up bowls, although the appearance may not be the height of conservatory fashion! This technique is very effective with well-growing plants in midsummer but should not be used in the spring, when roots are not well established. Likewise, by autumn, the pots should be removed from the water to start drying off the roots and commencing their dormancy.

WATER PLANTS

Cannas are naturally inhabitants of damp, marshy places. In particular *C. glauca* is found growing in swampy conditions in the West Indies and South America. It is, therefore, no surprise to discover that they not only thrive with copious water but that many will grow in damp waterside conditions and even in shallow water. Those that are generally called water cannas are hybrids derived from *C. glauca* crossed with other hybrids. They were developed by Robert J. Armstrong at the Longwood Gardens in the USA in the 1970s.

In gardens, *C. glauca* and all the closely-related water cannas can be grown as bog plants in wet soil at the side of a pool or can be planted in baskets and grown as marginals, with up to 15cm (6in) water above the rootstock. They do best when water temperatures are higher in hot summers and in a shallow pool that warms up quickly or in a pool or tank in a conservatory. Like all cannas, they need full sun to perform properly.

Other ordinary or terrestrial cannas have been successfully grown in water in various locations. One grower I know of uses traditional large-leaved cultivars, such as 'Wyoming' and 'Assaut'. Five or six plants are planted up into a large crate, approximately 50 × 60cm (18 × 24in), of the type used for carrying plants in nurseries. The crate is lined and filled as described below and then submerged in water. The result is quite stunning.

The soft, bluish foliage of *C. glauca* is a perfect foil for the delicate primrose-yellow flowers.

POTTING

Water cannas ideally require a basket of the sort used for planting aquatics. One at least 30cm (12in) across will be adequate for one good clump. It should be filled with a loam-based compost; peat-based compost is too light for water plants – they will tip over and may even float! Slow-release fertilizers of the type intended for water lilies can be added. The basket is normally lined with hessian or an artificial fabric before filling with soil and the clump is planted at the normal height. The surface is covered with a layer of gravel or chunky cobbles. These help to give the basket stability when the canna is eventually in full growth and they also prevent ducks or other water foragers from disturbing the soil until the plant is well rooted.

After planting, the baskets are initially stood in shallow water until the plants are acclimatized. They can then be submerged until as much as 15cm (6in) of water covers the roots. Theoretically, such submerged roots should not be at risk from frost because of the protective layer of water above them, but it is a wise precaution to take the baskets under cover for the winter as with other cannas. Water cannas do not seem to mind a certain degree of drying, although they prefer to be kept gently growing.

If you do not have a pool, you may wish to try growing water cannas in mini-ponds, which can be created in large watertight containers, such as ceramic planters. This makes an interesting variation on a terrace planter. Potted specimens of water cannas, together with other compact aquatics, are plunged into the water-filled container. The water will need constantly topping up in dry and warm weather and may need changing if it becomes stagnant. Such a display must be considered as a temporary feature and replanted each year. At the very least the container would probably crack in winter frosts.

WATERSIDES AND BOGS

The same canna varieties can also be grown very effectively at the waterside in soils which are constantly moist, along with other bog plants. In all of these aquatic situations, the cannas should still not be planted outside until early summer, when all danger of frost has passed.

PESTS AND DISEASES

Cannas are amazingly free from pests and diseases, although there are a few that do attack and can eventually cause serious damage. The incidence of pests and diseases varies with climatic conditions. For example, British gardens do not suffer from canna leaf-roller caterpillars, nor have I seen canna rust.

Most of the pests listed are most commonly found when cannas are grown in greenhouses for extended periods. Greenhouse conditions are favourable to the pest as well as the plant and, left unchecked, a small outbreak can rapidly become a major problem resulting in serious damage.

There is usually a choice of controls for the various pests. Where traditional spraying is carried out, the emphasis is usually on repeated applications at regular intervals. Greenhouses are also ideal for fumigation and this is a very efficient, albeit expensive, way of controlling many pests. It is also much easier to light a smoke bomb and retire quickly for a gin and tonic than spend a couple of hours inside a sticky spray suit with a heavy sprayer on one's back.

There are now many biological controls available for a wide range of pests and these are far more environmentally acceptable than traditional chemicals. Biological controls involve the use of a predator or parasite that kills the pest. For them to be effective, it is usually essential that they are employed from the beginning of a season, and chemicals cannot be used after they are in place as they might harm them. With all systems of biological control, there remains a low level of pest infestation, which serves to keep the predator or parasite alive. This is usually low enough that there is little discernible damage.

PESTS
Aphids

Greenfly and blackfly need little introduction, although the damage they cause is often underrated. Their sap-sucking always weakens the plant and the secreted honeydew leads to disfigurement and sooty mould. It is also important to control them as they act as vectors for viruses. Although they only occasionally attack cannas and generally only under glass, they can be persistent and difficult to control as they tend to hide within the furled young leaves, making spraying difficult. Sometimes aphids will suddenly appear on cannas in the early summer as they migrate from another plant species, and such abrupt appearances should be dealt with quickly, otherwise they can build up quickly to epidemic proportions.

There are many products for controlling aphids, some of the most effective being those containing pirimicarb. Soft soap products are environmentally more acceptable. Nowadays, there is a variety of biological controls among which the predator *Aphidoletes* is probably the most useful to use with cannas.

Whitefly

The greenhouse whitefly generally only attacks plants growing in greenhouses. Whitefly are also sap-sucking and cause damage which is similar to that caused by aphids. In general, this pest is very difficult to control as it has become resistant to most of the commonly available pesticides. Effective chemical control is based on repeated sprays at about four-day intervals, aiming to break the life cycle, which is extremely short. Alternating chemicals is also a valuable manoeuvre in the onslaught.

The commonest biological control for whitefly is the predator *Encarsia*, although there are others, and the more recent *Orius* may be valuable as it also preys on other pests such as aphids.

Slugs and Snails

These two well-known pests should be expected both under glass and outside. They thrive in wet seasons and in the damp conditions of a greenhouse where there are no natural predators such as birds. Cannas seem to be particularly attractive to slugs and snails and can be totally devastated by them. Unless you control them, expect young leaves to unfurl with cut patterns like a child's paper-tearing exercise!

Traditional slug pellets are the most effective control. Remember to scatter pellets around the young plants as the new growth is emerging in the greenhouse in the spring, before damage occurs. Plants that have been overwintered outside under a protective mulch are also vulnerable. This is because the mulch also provides the ideal home for overwintering slugs and snails. As soon as the new growth emerges, they have an instant food source – scatter slug pellets around the dormant clumps in early spring! Always apply slug pellets carefully, making sure that they do not lodge in the young furled leaves or the angles between leaf and stem. Pellets trapped in this way can cause scorch on the foliage.

There are various non-chemical ways of controlling slugs and snails, including a natural product containing an eelworm that parasitises them.

Red Spider Mite

Probably the most serious pest of cannas kept permanently under glass is the greenhouse red spider mite, which will also infect cucumbers, houseplants and a

'Stadt Fellbach' is among the better of the older compact cultivars and is good for planters as well as borders.

wide range of ornamentals in similar conditions. Initially, the symptoms are like a peppering of tiny yellow dots over the foliage, caused by the pest as it feeds under the leaf. This usually goes unnoticed until the populations are high and then the pest is difficult to control.

When dealing with red spider mite, it is advisable to remove as much of the remnants of last year's dried up stems as possible at the beginning of each new season: these are one of the places where the pest will have overwintered. A damp atmosphere, which is achieved with regular damping down, will also help to deter it.

Red spider mite seems to attack some cultivars more than others. If you have a few badly infested plants, it may be worthwhile cutting these back in mid-season and destroying the infested foliage to avoid the outbreak spreading to other plants. Cannas will usually easily recover from such harsh treatment, although it is unlikely that they will make sufficient growth to come back into flower the same season. Where traditional sprays are used and there have been bad attacks in previous seasons, spraying should start early, before damage is seen.

A predatory mite called *Phytoseilus* can be used during the summer months. Predators must be introduced early in the season before the pest becomes well established and cannot be combined with most other chemical sprays, although environmentally friendly products such as soft soap may be used to control other pests.

Mice

Mice can occasionally be troublesome in winter, when they eat the stored rhizomes. This is another reason for checking over cannas in store in the winter. Setting traps or using a poisoned bait is the only solution.

Caterpillars

In Britain, various caterpillars may sometimes attack cannas in midsummer. The damage they cause can easily be mistaken for slug attack as both pests leave holes in the leaves.

In southern states of the USA, from Texas to New York, the canna leaf-roller (*Calpodes ethlius*) is a serious pest. The caterpillar stage of the Brazilian skipper butterfly, this feeds on the upper surfaces of the leaves or on the unfurled leaves. The leaves are frayed, tattered

and shot full of holes, eventually the plants are defoliated and growth is severely checked. To shelter, the caterpillar fastens the damaged edges of the leaves together with silk to form a protective enclosure. When fully grown, it pupates inside a filmy cocoon. In some areas, cannas cannot be grown without regular spraying against this pest. The cultivar 'Wyoming' is particularly susceptible and for this reason is rarely grown in warm climates.

For all caterpillars, chemical control using various products such as those containing fenitrothion is possible. The biological control *Bacillus thuringiensis* is also effective against caterpillars.

Sciarid Flies

This pest is prevalent where cannas are grown in loamless composts with a high level of peat or other organic matter. It is generally only a problem under greenhouse conditions and usually disappears when the cannas are planted outside. The adult pest is a tiny black fly and clouds of these will rise from the compost surface when it is disturbed by watering or other movement. The larval stage, which lives under the surface of the compost, feeds on plant roots. It may go unnoticed until plants collapse due to total loss of roots. It is particularly bad in the early months of the year when growth is slow or with plants that are sluggish.

Spraying with soft soap and other insecticides will control adults, which effectively breaks the life cycle. To kill the larvae, it is necessary to drench the compost with a solution of malathion, made up to 50 per cent of the normal strength. Alternatively there is a biological control that utilizes a beneficial eelworm that parasitizes the sciarid larvae.

Vine Weevil

A very wide range of plants are attacked by vine weevils, and cannas are not exempt. Vine weevils can be difficult to eradicate and are easily imported on new plants, either swapped from other collectors or from commercial growers. The adult is a relatively harmless brown beetle-like bug that crawls around and may eat a few notches from the lower leaves. The larva, however, is a voracious feeder and lives underground destroying

Fortunately, canna leaf-roller is not found in temperate climates, but in some countries it decimates the foliage.

plant roots. It is easily recognized as a small, fat, curled grub, about 5–10mm (¼–½) long, that is white with a darker head. Fortunately, the regular growing cycle of cannas, whereby they are divided annually, means that grubs are usually detected at the dividing and potting stage and can be washed off the rhizomes and destroyed. Both chemical drenches and a biological treatment are available.

Nematodes

Root knot eelworms (*Meloidogyne* species) have been identified as attacking cannas but there are no records of them being a major problem.

DISEASES
Canna Rust

Canna rust (*Puccinia thaliae*) is virtually unknown in temperate areas, but in hot, humid climates, where it does affect cannas, it produces orange-coloured pustules, like gold dust, on the lower surface of the leaves leading to unsightly blackening and die-back. It is spread from spores, which are splashed up from the ground onto the lower leaves when it rains. It is much more rife in hot, wet conditions. Where it is prevalent, control should be by means of a protective fungicidal spray in advance of the appearance of the disease, which is very difficult to eradicate once established. Spraying the mulch or soil around the plants is also effective. In a bad attack it may be prudent to cut the affected plants to the ground and allow them to re-grow. Infected leaves must be destroyed.

Rhizome Rots

Decay of the rhizomes may occur either in storage or in the early part of the year soon after planting. It may be caused by fungal species of genera such as *Sclerotinium*, *Fusarium* or *Pythium* or the bacteria *Erwinia*, which causes similar symptoms. A cottony fungal growth may be present in the decaying rhizome and there may also be an unpleasant smell.

To avoid problems in the first place, care should be taken to avoid damaging the rhizomes and to trim all broken parts cleanly. On a commercial scale, chemical fungicides may be used, either at the planting stage or during storage. This latter treatment is less acceptable nowadays as the rhizome will be handled by the consumer when planting. On the home garden scale, sul-

phur fungicides can be used during storage but are not normally necessary at any other time.

Bacterial Bud Rot

This disease causes decay and death of both shoots and leaves but is not particularly prevalent.

Grey Mould

Caused by the fungus *Botrytis cinerea*, grey mould is generally only seen on canna flowers as they decay. It is likely to be more prevalent under damp conditions or where spent flowers do not fall freely, when it will occur in the decaying flower and may spread to unopened buds. Treatment is generally by good hygiene, removing old flowers as they fade.

Fungal Leaf Spot

This is caused by a species of *Alternaria* but does not occur regularly and is usually of no major importance.

Viruses

Viruses are not widespread as yet, although any distorted or spotted growth is best treated as virus and the plants destroyed. There are several possible viruses and it is sometimes difficult to be sure that distorted cannas actually are suffering from a virus and, for most gardeners, very complicated to identify which one: in most cases, it requires a laboratory and an electron microscope. In general, dark-leaved cultivars seem to be less susceptible to canna viruses, although it is possible that the foliage colour masks some of the symptoms.

Bean yellow mosaic, which causes a chlorotic mosaic pattern on the leaves, has a wide host range, including commercial crops such as peas, beans and clover. It is, therefore, probably distributed worldwide. Most cultivars seem to have a level of resistance to it and given good growing conditions will grow, thrive and flower despite the infection.

Hippeastrum mosaic has a wide host range. On cannas it shows as crinkled foliage and chlorotic streaking. It weakens susceptible plants and can cause death. 'Wyoming' and 'Ambassador' are said to be very resistant, which possibly explains why such old cultivars have survived so well.

Canna yellow mottle is the most dangerous of the viruses, although co-infection with other viruses often exists, masking its true effects. First reported in Japan in 1985, it shows as a foliar chlorosis and necrotic mottling. Put simply this means that there are yellow streaks that eventually turn to brown patches. It is present in canna stocks, particularly in the USA and Japan, but may be more widely spread.

There is no control for viruses and, as they can easily spread to other cannas, any plants that are suspected of infection should be destroyed immediately by burning, or at the very least isolated. Viruses are generally spread by insect vectors, such as aphids, and it is, therefore, important to keep plants free of these pests. If plants have uncertain symptoms that could possibly be virus, it is important to keep them separate until identification can be certain.

A WORD OF WARNING!

There are now few restrictions on the movement of plants within the EU and in 1998 a major exchange of cannas was arranged between the National Collection in Britain, which I look after, and a serious plant collector in Europe. There was no requirement for inspection and growing plants were supplied in pots. As the plants grew, I became aware of peculiar leaf speckling and general sickliness. Initially, I assumed this to be a physiological reaction to new conditions but the plants failed to grow away healthily. The Royal Horticultural Society at Wisley could not identify the problem and so samples went to the Central Science Laboratory for electron microscope identification. They identified both canna yellow mottle and bean yellow mosaic. The result was that I had to destroy some 50 new cultivars to avoid the disease spreading to the rest of the stock.

To prevent infection of existing stock, any new plants from unknown sources, whether from abroad or not, should always be grown separately until one is sure of their health. (For more information on importing and exporting cannas see appendix 4, p.153.)

Canna 'Assaut' in a formal bedding display with *Dahlia* 'Moonfire', helichrysums and begonias.

4

PROPAGATION

Most gardeners want to increase favourite plants, and the propagation of cannas is very simple. In my experience of selling canna plants, the customer often asks how many plants the clump will make in future years and is encouraged to know that this year's clump will usually yield a minimum of three new plants the very next year.

DIVISION

Dividing is the mostly commonly used method of increasing cannas, particularly if you have existing clumps that you wish to propagate. These clumps may have been lifted from the garden in the autumn and stored under cover, they may be potted specimens or, in mild areas, they may still be in the soil, having been left outside all winter.

Whatever the source, some of the soil or compost will need to be carefully knocked or washed off the old clump in order to locate the shoots and eyes. Plants that have been kept in large pots may have become quite congested and the pot may be distorted with the growth of the rhizomes. If the pot is a cheap plastic one, it may be prudent to cut it off rather than damage the plant. Sometimes rhizomes will have dropped to the base of the pot and may be appearing through the drainage holes. In this case, dismantling the pot completely is the only way to release the plant.

Some gardeners choose to divide cannas when they are totally dormant but there are distinct advantages to waiting until young growth has just started. Firstly, the new shoots will be easier to identify, and secondly,

once growth has started, with new root action, there is less chance of the divisions rotting. With potted cannas, it is advantageous to start the plants into growth before dividing them as new shoots can then clearly be seen. The initial watering in this case must wet all parts of the root ball. The compost, which will shrink when dry, may have reduced to the extent that the water just runs down between the pot-and the root ball. It may, therefore, be necessary to fill this void with a little new compost to help retain the water. Loamless composts, in particular, can be very difficult to re-wet; a few drops of a wetting agent such as soft soap added to the water can help this process.

MAKING THE DIVISIONS

With some types of cannas, such as 'Strasbourg', it may be possible to pull apart mother clumps into smaller sections. However, with many, the clumps will be too congested and all parts of the rhizome are connected so a sharp knife will have to be used to cut the plant up. Remember that, for a division to grow into a new plant, it must have at least one shoot or viable dormant growing point. For most garden purposes a division with three to five shoots, or eyes, will be the most useful, forming a well-balanced plant. However, when large quantities of plants are required, it may be desirable to divide the rhizomes into single eyes. Amazingly these small divisions often grow fast, develop other shoots from the base of the original and make quite presentable clumps by the end of the season.

POTTING

The young divisions need to be grown on in pots until they can be planted out. Cannas will grow in almost

Low-growing daisies, including *Osteospermum*, make a carpet around the strong foliage and bright flowers of C. 'Assaut'.

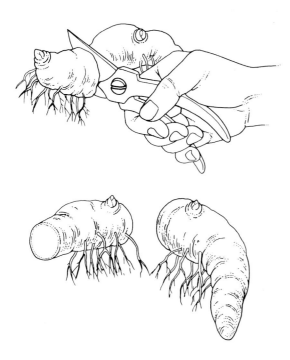

Canna rhizomes are divided using secateurs or a knife and leaving a bud on each section.

any type of good potting compost but they do seem to respond particularly well to open, loamless composts. For many years, I have used a coarse grade of loamless compost of the type designed for nursery stock production. This is particularly well-drained, which avoids stagnation of the compost in the early weeks before the canna roots are growing vigorously. The nutrients in such composts last only a few weeks, however, and must be followed up with liquid feeding on a regular basis. Alternatively, something that works very well with cannas is to mix a balanced slow-release fertilizer in with the compost before potting. Choose one with a release period of around three months – a longer-lasting product will be wasted.

The size of pot to be used will vary with the size of the rhizome. Small rhizomes with only one shoot may be quite happy in a 12.5cm (5in) pot. For most purposes, 15–20cm (6–9in) pots are best and adequate for a 3–5-eye clump. In general, do not overpot at the initial stage as the compost easily stagnates and the roots may rot. Better to move on later to a larger pot. Beyond that there are no rules: old clumps that have

been saved from year to year may have grown quite large and require much bigger pots.

Place the roots in the pot so that they are just covered, but not excessively buried. Any shoots that are visible should be left above the compost level. After potting, give the compost a light watering to settle the roots in. Subsequent watering should be very light as root growth is slow to start with and there are no leaves to take water out of the compost. Overwatering can easily result in the compost staying cold and wet, which may lead to the rhizomes rotting.

Where space is at a premium, canna rhizomes can be potted in smaller pots initially and moved on to larger sizes as growth develops. They have the bad habit of producing their shoots to one side of the pot, so an advantage of this technique is that at the potting-on stage, the plant can be centred in the larger pot. Alternatively, two or three similar small plants can be moved into a large pot to make a balanced specimen. Cannas can also be started temporarily in trays, a technique that is very useful if you have stock of uncertain viability. Many divisions can be loosely fitted into a tray of compost and as soon as growth is evident, they can be divided further and then potted up.

It is quite possible to divide cannas later in the spring, when they are in full leaf, if reasonable care is taken. This may simply be to provide a plant as a gift for an admirer, in which case a suitable side shoot, with a portion of rhizome and roots, can be removed from the main plant. Small shoots with two or three leaves are ideal for this, although larger shoots can be used if the top growth is reduced. Such divisions will need to be carefully nurtured until re-established, by shading or possibly shrouding with polythene to reduce water loss. Larger, in-leaf divisions are possible, but great care must be taken to avoid them wilting.

TEMPERATURES
Newly potted cannas must be kept in a frost-free greenhouse: this is the minimum requirement. A temperature of 10°C (50°F) is the optimum and encourages steady but not lush growth. Higher temperatures tend to result in soft growth, which can easily be damaged or topple over. Perhaps the ideal is to start cannas on a heated bench with a soil warming cable or pad underneath the pots. This should be set to achieve a root zone temperature of around 16–21°C (60–70°F) with

Young cannas soon after dividing, growing in a polytunnel with a propane heater.

the greenhouse air temperature at 10°C (50°F). A warm rooting zone will stimulate the growth of new fibrous roots and discourage any decay organisms. As soon as the new roots start to absorb water and nutrients from the compost, shoot growth will follow. Once steady growth has commenced, the pots can be moved from the heated bench to the ordinary greenhouse environment to grow on steadily. A variation on this treatment, and one which maximizes the use of space, is to pack the divided roots into trays on a heated bench and then to pot the plants up as soon as growth has started.

Many amateur growers have great success with raising cannas in minimally heated structures, such as polythene tunnels, using basic techniques and a minimum of equipment and expenditure. Some heating is still necessary to prevent freezing, although by delaying potting until mid-spring, even this can be avoided.

After potting, the tunnel is kept closed on all but the hottest days. The radiant heat of the sun will be absorbed by the dark surface of the compost and the warmth will stimulate early root growth. Although very high air temperatures will occur inside the tunnel, there is no risk of scorching as there is initially no shoot growth. Watering under such conditions must be particularly sparing at the commencement to avoid rotting of the rhizomes before roots have formed. If very low night-time temperatures are predicted, the pots and emerging shoots should be covered with horticultural fleece, which must be removed each day.

Once shoots do start to appear, some ventilation is allowed but temperatures well up to 30°C (86°F) seem to do no harm; watering can also be increased. Cannas do, of course, originate from very hot climates and seem to be able to adapt to widely fluctuating temperatures between day and night.

With such late starting there will be little visible growth before late spring but once roots are formed and the first shoots emerge, the speed of growth increases rapidly. Amazingly, plants grown in this way almost seem to catch up with others that have been started under more conventional conditions and specimens will have achieved quite an acceptable size by planting-out time in early summer.

GROWING ON

Once cannas have started to make good leaf growth, the compost will dry out much more rapidly and watering will need to be increased. On warm spring days, it may be necessary to water cannas that are in full growth twice a day. At each watering, sufficient water must be applied to thoroughly wet the compost throughout the pot. If a plant appears not to be thriving, it is well worth checking whether the bottom of the root zone is remaining dry after watering.

As natives of warm countries, cannas appreciate bright sunlight. They should, therefore, be grown in a light part of the greenhouse. Under greenhouse conditions, it is rarely necessary to shade them from the sun. The only exception is when keeping them under glass for flowering, when it can be helpful to provide light shading to prolong the life of the individual flowers.

FEEDING

With loamless composts, if a slow-release fertilizer has not been added at the potting stage, supplementary feeding will usually be necessary. This is normally started about four weeks after potting, although the precise recommendations of the compost's manufacturer should be noted. The need for nutrients is also dependent on the amount of watering that has taken place; where this has been minimal, there may be no need to start feeding until somewhat later. Some growers report success with foliar feeding but before carrying this out on a large scale, a small trial should be made to ensure that there are no problems with scorch.

Little else is necessary during the spring months under glass. A watch must be kept for pests and diseases, however, as these are especially prevalent under glass (see pp.00–00). In particular, slug control should be considered if there is any likelihood of damage. At this stage, when there is little foliage, a slug attack can decimate young plants. Depending on the initial spacing of the pots in the greenhouse, it may also be necessary to space them out to allow more light between the plants and to avoid them becoming spindly. Plants

with single shoots and those planted late will usually have enough room to develop when grown 'pot thick' (without extra spacing); however, plants with several shoots and those that have been started early, will certainly need extra space. The ideal is that spacing should be such that leaves do not touch, although there is rarely enough space in most greenhouses to be quite so generous.

GROWING FROM SEED

Canna seed is like a small dark ball-bearing, very comparable to the more familiar sweet pea seed. Similarly, it has a very hard seed coat, which no doubt gave rise to the canna's common name, Indian shot plant. Most keen gardeners like to try growing plants from seed and it is quite possible to grow some cannas in this way. Cannas from seed can be most rewarding and many will flower in their first season, given an early start: this should be between late winter and mid-spring according to the conditions available. It is better, however, to wait until later, if conditions are likely to be too cold.

It must be emphasized that most cannas do not breed true from seed. Seeds saved from large-flowered hybrids may well produce a selection of quite presentable offspring but, however similar they may appear to their parents, they should never be assumed to be the same or given the same cultivar name. Genetically they are likely to be different and may have different traits, such as lack of hardiness or less disease resistance, which are not so readily discernible. In general, the canna species are more likely to breed true from seed than the hybrids, although this is only certain where the plants are grown in isolation or come from a native source. Mixed canna seed is available from some seed houses and is likely to produce an acceptable batch of varied plants. There are also a few named strains, such as 'Tropical Rose' and 'Tropical Red', that will produce more predictable results.

SCARIFICATION

If sown with no prior preparation, canna seed is usually very slow and sporadic in germination and the percentage success rate is likely to be low. Various techniques have been developed for improving germination by breaking through the hard outer coat and allowing moisture to enter. This is scarification. The soundest technique for small quantities of seed is to nick the seed

The bright yellow flowers of 'Richard Wallace' are freely produced throughout the season.

coat carefully with either a small nail file or hacksaw blade until the paler inner tissues are just visible. Sandpaper can also be used. Holding the seeds with a pair of pliers makes the job a little easier, but this is tedious work and care has to be taken not to cause a hand injury. After scarification, the seed is soaked for 48 hours in warm water before sowing. Any seed that floats should be discarded as it is unlikely to be viable. The remainder should now be swollen and can be sown as described below.

THE HOT-WATER TECHNIQUE

With larger quantities of seed, or for those with less patience, the hot-water technique can be tried. Place the seed in a small bowl and pour hot water over it. The water should be just off the boil, about 70–80°C (158–176°F). Leave the seed in the hot water for about 20 minutes. It can then either be further soaked for two or three days or sown immediately. Some growers like to remove the now softened darker outer case before sowing but this is a messy business and not essential.

The hot-water technique is not as reliable as mechanical scarification, as it can be tricky to judge the temperature of the water. There is a risk that the soaking will not be effective or that, if the water is too hot, the seed will be killed. Despite this, some growers have mastered the trick and find it very successful. It is not recommended for small quantities of valuable seed.

SOWING

As canna seeds are quite large, they can be sown directly into a potting compost, although a seed-sowing compost is equally acceptable. The seed can be broadcast, spacing it carefully in trays of compost, but the ideal is to sow it individually in small modules or peat blocks. It should be covered with about 5mm (¼in) of compost. The seed containers are then covered with a sheet of black plastic to exclude the light and to help retain moisture. Heat is required for germination, so the containers should be placed in a seed propagator or wherever the compost temperature can be maintained at around 21°C (70°F).

The trays should be should be checked daily for germinating seedlings. If the compost is dry, it should be carefully watered, and the black polythene should be turned before replacing it to avoid the condensation making the surface too wet. With the correct conditions, seed will usually germinate fast and evenly within a few days. As soon as the first shoots are observed, the polythene must be removed and the seedlings placed in a light position. In very bright sunlight, a little shading may be necessary for the first few days until the seedlings are green and acclimatized to the surrounding conditions. As cannas are monocotyledons, there will be just one single narrow initial leaf.

Seedlings from broadcast seed will have to be pricked out at an early stage before the brittle young roots tangle. Once the primary leaf is about 2.5cm (1in) long, they are easy to handle. Each plant should be levered up gently with a dibber or old table fork and moved into a small pot or module of its own filled with a good

'Journey's End' is readily available, particularly in the USA. It is variable in height, but usually short.

potting compost. A dibber should be used to make a large hole for the copious and fragile roots, which should be firmed gently into place. The young plants should be gently watered in, using a watering can with a fine rose, and shaded for a couple of days with paper or fleece if the sun is very bright.

Seedlings need to be grown on at a minimum of 10°C (50°F), although a higher temperature is preferable, ideally nearer to 16°C (60°F). Once growth is vigorous, the young plants can be progressively potted on into 9cm (3½in) and then 12.5cm (5in) pots, and the temperature can be reduced. When growing species, such as C. 'Warszewiczii', or single colours, such as 'Tropical Rose', three seedlings can be planted into one pot to make a bigger, more rounded plant in a shorter space of time. They are grown on in a similar way to other cannas and then planted out in the garden for their summer display. If sown early and grown generously, most cannas should flower in their first season. Although they will produce rhizomes at the end of the summer,

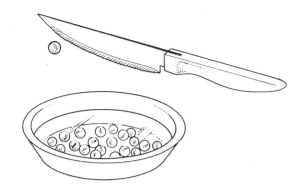

After scarifying with a small file or knife, the canna seeds are soaked in warm water.

these may be small and will need overwintering carefully to avoid desiccation.

HARDENING OFF

Before they are planted out, like all tender plants, cannas need to be hardened off to acclimatize them to the outdoor temperatures of late spring. Traditionally, this involves moving plants to a coldframe and gradually increasing the ventilation until the plants are accustomed to outdoor conditions. Few gardeners have coldframes nowadays, so this will usually mean increasing the ventilation in a greenhouse or polytunnel until it is as near as possible the same inside and out, day and night. When just a few plants are involved, these can be moved outside on warm, sunny days and returned to the greenhouse at night until all danger of frost is past and they can be left outside ready for planting.

MICROPROPAGATION

Micropropagation is a modern technique used for producing vast numbers of young plants under laboratory conditions. However, it is not very successful with cannas. Initially there is a problem in obtaining sterile tissue from the growing points of cannas, as these are located at soil level and usually contaminated with various organisms. In instances where this difficulty has been successfully overcome, there is a later problem as the young plantlets do not multiply at an economically viable rate. The technique has, however, been used for the production of the Island Series of cannas.

Seeds are then planted in small pots of compost in warm conditions, where they will grow rapidly.

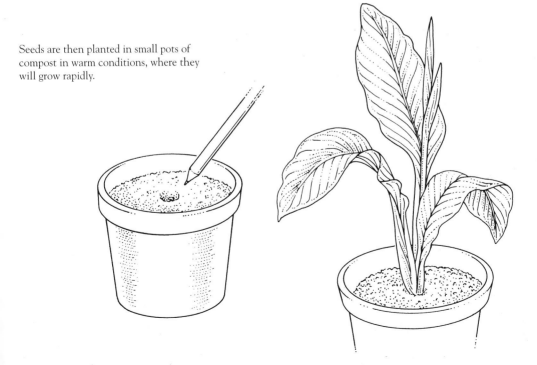

5

CANNA SPECIES

As with many groups of plants that have been highly cultivated for a long period of time, cannas suffer from problems with nomenclature. In part this comes from the cultural nature of the plant. In temperate climates, they must be planted, lifted, stored, moved from store to greenhouse, divided and moved back outside every year. The whole process gives numerous opportunities for lost labels. Then, as with any other plant, there are misnamings due to ignorance by both gardeners and professionals and occasionally blatant misnaming for commercial reasons by nurserymen. It has also been said that the founder of one major American canna company had such strong political affinities that he renamed one canna because it commemorated an American senator who was not of his own political persuasion!

The canna is also relatively easily grown from seed, and such seedlings have often been given the names of their parents or of other cannas that they resemble. Such seed-grown plants always differ in some ways, however small, from their ancestors, and the result, over a period of time, is that stocks can be very variable. This may account for cultivars such as 'President', 'Fireside' and 'Oiseau de Feu' which, for ordinary garden purposes, are identical but between which, if minute examination is carried out, distinctions can be made. I am often asked to identify from photographs cannas growing in a distant country. I do not think that it is possible to say that a certain canna is categorically the same as an identical-looking cultivar grown in Britain. Although plants may have been imported to

that country at some stage in the past, it is equally likely that a similar cultivar has been developed from an independent breeding programme. If that is the case, the plant, however similar it may appear, will have a different genetic constitution and cannot be called the same as its British 'look-alike'.

HISTORICAL NAMING PROBLEMS

It would seem that nomenclature of cannas has always been the subject of debate. Old journals give various complicated keys and divisions into subgenera, such as *Eucanna, Distemon, Eurostylus* and *Achiridia*, which are not accepted today. Classification schemes are also listed for the garden hybrids, with cultivars described as gladiolus-flowered, orchid-flowered or iris-flowered. The most detailed attempt at classification seems to be in a paper in *The Gardeners' Chronicle* of 7 October 1893. This puts forward an initial division into dwarf cultivars, not exceeding 20in (50cm) and tall cultivars that exceed 20in (50cm), with both divisions then subdivided into green foliage and purple foliage. Each subdivision is further split into five groups relating to flower description. The first group includes 'self-coloured', with just one colour to the entire flower. The second is 'bicolour forms', where one petal or the lip is of a different colour. The third comprises 'spotted cultivars' and the fourth 'blotched forms'. Finally, 'margined forms' are separated. Nowhere is there any reference to the gladiolus, orchid and iris form used by other authorities. This classification also lacks a convenient slot for pencilled or lined cultivars. It seems safe to hazard a guess that classification of cannas fell apart because of the inability to agree a common format for splitting them.

The delicate flowers of C. *iridiflora* 'Ehemanii' set within a carpet of sweet-scented heliotrope.

In 1923, the American Joint Committee on Horticultural Nomenclature produced a list of standardized plant names, which included a number of cannas. It is interesting to see that even then synonyms and 'unapproved' names were in use. *In Evolution of Cultivated Cannas*, Khoshoo and Guha suggest with a possible family tree (see opposite).

CANNA SPECIES

Older books contain lists of 60 or more species of *Canna*; however, recent taxonomic studies have suggested that there are no more than 10 distinct wild species, although there are numerous cultivars and hybrids. While there are many small-flowered cannas available from nurseries in Britain and overseas with species-type names, sadly very few of the recently validated species are available, either from the nursery trade or even in botanic gardens.

TAXONOMIC RESEARCH

The most recent work on *Canna* species has been carried out by Paul and Hiltje Maas in Holland. Professor Dr P. J. M. Maas has been interested in the Cannaceae family since 1971, when a preliminary systematic treatment of the Cannaceae of northern South America was published, based on a student research project. His main interest at that time were Costaceae and Zingiberaceae, groups of distantly related monocotyledonous herbs. Since then he (and his wife) have been studying wild *Canna* species all over tropical America during many field trips. As a result, they have compiled a large collection of herbarium sheets, alcohol collections, slides and literature on Cannaceae at the Utrecht Herbarium in the Netherlands.

I am indebted to Dr Hiltje Maas, who has provided considerable help with this section on wild species of *Canna*. I have not attempted to change the botanical style of writing but have added my own comments underneath where the species are available and used for ornamental display.

C. bangii Kraenzl.

Plants to 4m (13ft) tall. Leaves green, lower side more or less lanuginose. Inflorescences repeatedly branched with persistent floral bracts; pedicel densely tuberculate just below the ovary or fruit. Flowers erect, oranged-red, 4–7cm (1½–3in) long, composed of 8 or more coloured parts; petals not reflexed; staminodes 3 or more. Found in Peru and Bolivia at an altitude of 1,400–2,700m (4,500–8,900ft).

Generally not available in cultivation.

C. flaccida Salisb.

Plants to 2m (7ft) tall; rhizomes horizontally creeping. Leaves green, lower side more or less glaucous, base gradually narrowing into the sheath, apex often ending in a filiform thread. Flowers erect, yellow, relatively large (10–14cm/4–5½in long), composed of 9 coloured parts; sepals acute; petals reflexed; staminodes 4, showy and flaccid, 1.5–6.5cm (½–2¾in) wide, margins undulate. Capsules 3–6cm (1¼–2⅜in) long, seeds 5–7mm (¼in) in diam. Found in south-eastern USA at sea level.

Originally introduced to cultivation in 1788, this species is available from collectors and botanic gardens and is worth growing for its curiosity value. Its flowers open at night and close in the heat of day, presenting a flaccid appearance, hence the name. It has the largest flowers among the wild species cannas except for those of *C. liliiflora*. In particular the lip of the flower is huge and wavy and this characteristic was recognized as valuable by nineteenth-century hybridists who used it as a parent of many of the early hybrid cannas that were originally known as orchid-flowered cannas.

C. glauca L.

Plants to 3m (10ft) tall, completely glaucous, growing in wet places, often bordering streams, almost aquatic; rhizomes long-creeping. Leaves green, glaucous, relatively narrow (1.5–14cm/½–5½in wide), base and apex very gradually narrowed. Flowers erect, yellow, 7–10cm (3–4in) long, composed of 9 coloured parts; petals not reflexed; staminodes 4. Found all over tropical America, generally at low elevations.

This species is generally available in private collections and from some specialist plant nurseries. It is a good garden plant, making a tall, willowy statement for the back of a border, and is particularly at home in wet areas by a pool or streamside. The narrow, glaucous foliage is well complemented by the delicate pale lemon-yellow flowers. It is also of interest as it has been used as a parent at various stages of canna breeding and most recently in the production of the 'water cannas' (p.39).

ORIGIN OF GARDEN CANNA
(after T.N. Khoshoo and I. Guha: *Evolution of Cultivated Cannas*)

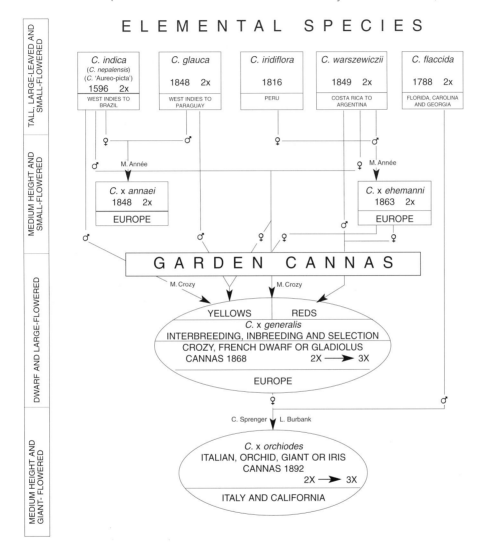

C. indica L.

Plants to 3m (10ft) tall in the wild. Leaves green, lower side smooth, sometimes lanuginose. Inflorescence often branched; pedicels not tuberculate; floral bracts persistent. Flowers erect, red to yellow, 4–6.5cm (1½–2¾in) long, composed of 8 or more coloured parts; staminodes 3 or more. Found throughout tropical America, up to altitudes of 2,000m (6,500ft).

The form available from specialist nurseries is quite a compact plant growing to no more than 1–1.5m (3–5ft) in cultivation. Under British conditions it is often one of the first to flower each year. This species is said to have been introduced to the British Isles by Gerard in 1596.

Various other cannas, previously classed as species in their own right, should now be included within this species, according to the international rules of taxonomic nomenclature. These include C. 'Achiras', C. 'Aurantiaca', C. 'Coccinea', C. 'Discolor', C. 'Esculenta', C. 'Edulis', C. 'Lanuginosa', C. 'Limbata', C. 'Lutea', C. 'Patens', C. 'Speciosa', and C. 'Warszewiczii'.

C. iridiflora Ruiz & Pav.

Plants to 5m (16ft) tall. Leaves green, plicate, lower side and sheaths often lanuginose. Inflorescence branched. Flowers pendent, carmine-red to purple, 10–14cm (4–5½in) long, with a relatively long tubular part and 8 coloured lobes; petals not reflexed; staminodes 4. Occurs in Peru at altitudes of 1,800–2,850m (6,000–9,000ft). It was introduced to Britain in 1816.

In cultivation, this species is most commonly represented by C. 'Ehemanii', a hybrid between C. iridiflora and C. 'Warzcewiczii', which is very similar but has a fuller inflorescence and narrower petals. It drops its flowers cleanly and never sets seed, unlike the species itself, which seeds copiously.

The original cross is believed to have been made by M. Année in 1863 and named after the French-German gardener Ehemann. However, various references seem to suggest that the cross has been repeated at various points in history with similar results. It is quite tough and tolerates more frost than many cannas. It flowers quite late and is, therefore, a splendid conservatory plant that can be appreciated well into the autumn months. Both the wild species and 'Ehemanii' will grow in semi-aquatic conditions.

C. jaegeriana Urb.

Plants to 5m (16ft) tall. Leaves green, lower side and sheaths more or less lanuginose. Inflorescence sometimes branched, pedicels 0–5mm (0–¼in) long, to 1cm (½in) in fruit; floral bracts caducous. Flowers erect, orange, 4–7.5cm (1½–3in) long, floral tube curved, composed of 9 or more coloured parts of about equal length; petals not reflexed; staminodes 4 or 5. Seeds narrowly ellipsoid and relatively small (4–6.5mm × 2–4mm/c.¼in). Found in western South America and Greater Antilles, generally growing at high altitudes (750–2,800m/2,500–9,000ft).

Occasionally seen in plant collections but not generally available.

C. liliiflora Warsz. ex Planch.

Plants to 6m (20ft) tall. Leaves green, large – 35–120cm × 20–45cm (14–48in × 8–18in), lower side and sheaths more or less lanuginose. Flowers erect, greenish-white, large (9–12.5cm/3½–5in long), composed of 9 coloured parts; petals reflexed; staminodes 4. Capsules 5–10.5cm (2–4¼in) long; seeds 8–10mm

(⅜–½in) in diameter. Occurs in Bolivia at an altitude of 2,500–2,800m (8,000–9,000ft).

This is the nearest to a white among the species cannas. Occasionally seen in plant collections, it is not generally available. Reports describe it as difficult to cultivate and dying out quickly in cultivation. This species is reported to be pollinated by bats and to have a herbaceous, soapy scent.

C. paniculata Ruiz & Pav.

Plants to 5m (16ft) tall. Leaves green, sessile or shortly but distinctly petiolate, petiole with pulvinus, lower side of leaves mostly lanuginose. Inflorescence often branched. Flowers erect, red to yellow or scarlet, 6–10cm (2½–4in) long, composed of 6 coloured parts of about equal length; petals not reflexed; staminode one. Found in southern Mexico, Costa Rica and tropical South America, except for the Amazon Basin at 200–2,000m (650–6,500ft).

Occasionally seen in plant collections but not generally available.

C. pedunculata Sims

Plants to 2.5m (8ft) tall. Leaves green, glaucous and relatively narrow (4–13cm/1½–5in wide). Flowers erect, yellow, relatively small (3–4cm/1¼–1½in long), composed of 9 coloured parts; sepals obtuse; petals reflexed; staminodes 4, narrow (2–10mm/¼–½in wide). Occurs in south-east Brazil at low altitudes.

Quite rare and unknown in most collections.

C. tuerckheimii Kraenzl.

Plants to 3.5m (11½ft) tall. Leaves green, relatively large – 30–100cm × 15–40cm (12–36in × 6–16in), lower side and sheaths more or less lanuginose. Inflorescence often branched; pedicels 0.5–3cm (¼–1¼in) long, to 4.5cm (1¾in) in fruit; floral bracts caducous. Flowers erect, orange-red, 5.5–9cm (2¼–3½in) long, floral tube not curved, composed of 9 coloured parts; petals not reflexed; staminodes 4. Occurs in Andean South America, and in Central America to Mexico at altitudes of 500–2,000m (1,600–6,500ft).

Occasionally seen in plant collections but not generally available.

NOTE

Scientific reports from Japan discuss the recent discovery of a number of new canna species in Argentina. These have been named C. *stenantha*, C. *jacobiniflora* and C. *amabilis* and were collected from swampy habitats in northern Argentina. There is also reference to C. *plurituberosa*. More details on these species are yet to be made available.

SPECIES OR NOT?

Those who are familiar with cannas will be wondering what has happened to a whole host of plants that are available in plant collections and generally cultivated throughout the world. Quite simply, although they are distinct plants, the current level of taxonomic research and interest is such that they cannot be given a definitive name and taxonomic status. This is not a new situation and one wonders whether it will ever be totally untangled. As early as 1789, botanists such as Willdenow and Aiton were recognizing cannas such as C. *coccinea*, C. *lutea*, C. *patens* and C. *rubra* as varieties of C. *indica*.

The unclassified cannas are listed below under the names generally given to them in horticultural situations. It is thought that most originated in cultivation at some stage, although they may now be naturalized in various areas. In order to distinguish them from the wild species cannas, the names are placed in inverted commas, although they are not ideal as cultivar names, as these should not be Latinised. Many of these cannas are correctly C. *indica* (see. p.57).

C. 'Achiras' (syn. C. 'Lanuginosa') This is an old name for C. 'Edulis'.

C. 'Aurantiaca' This is a form of C. 'Lutea'.

C. 'Coccinea' Quite an attractive plant with wavy green leaves and small red flowers. It is reasonably tough and makes a valid background plant. It is like a taller version of C. 'Warszewiczii' and grows to about 1.8m (6ft).

C. 'Discolor' Said to be a native of Central America, this was introduced in 1872. It has green leaves, up to 90cm (36in) long and 30cm (12in) wide, with purple margins and undersides. Flowers are red, yellow and purple. It grows to about 1.8m (6ft). (See also C. *indica*.)

'Heliconifolia' is generally grown for its foliage, but close-up the flowers are quite delicate.

C. 'Esculenta' See C.*indica*.

C. 'Heliconifolia' A very tall canna, growing to over 2.4m (8ft). It bears pale orange flowers but for garden display should be considered as a foliage plant. It is more commonly seen as the slightly improved cultivar 'Omega'.

C. 'Indica Purpurea' There are several versions of this fabulous foliage plant. It has a slender habit, rich purple leaves and small, upright, orange flowers. Although the name is doubtful, this is a very widely grown canna making an excellent foliage statement. It can reach up to over 2.1m (7ft) and seems to be one of the hardier types, tolerant of overwintering in the ground. The

KEY TO THE SPECIES OF CANNA

Botanical keys provide a valuable way of identifying unknown plants via a series of planned steps. The key must be followed quite precisely and a knowledge of botanical terms is required. The use of a magnifying glass is also often essential to verify certain floral characteristics.

This key is printed by kind permission of Paul and Hiltje Maas.

1. Staminode one; flower composed of six coloured parts (3 petals, 1 style, 1 stamen, 1 staminode); leaves shortly but distinctly petiolate and thickened, lower side mostly lanuginose.
Identify as **C. paniculata** Ruiz & Pav.
or
1. Staminodes three or more; flower composed of eight or more coloured parts. Go to 2.

2. Cultivated plants with large, showy flowers and green or reddish-brown leaves.
Identify as **C. × generalis** (garden forms of canna) L. H. Bailey.
or
2. Wild plants with green leaves. Go to 3.

3. Petals reflexed; flowers greenish-white or yellow. **Go to 4.**
or
3. Petals not reflexed; flowers red, orange, or yellow. **Go to 6.**

4. Flowers greenish-white; capsules 5–10cm (2–4in) long, seeds 8–10mm (⅜–½in) in diameter.
Identify as **C. liliiflora** Warsz. ex Planch.
or
4. Flowers yellow; capsules 3–6cm (1½–2½in) long, seeds 5–7mm (³⁄₁₆–⁵⁄₁₆in) in diameter. **Go to 5.**

5. Flowers 10–14cm (4–5½in) long; staminodes 1.5–6.5cm (¾–3½in) wide; sepals acute.
Identify as **C. flaccida** Salisb.
or
5. Flowers 3–4cm (1¼–1½in) long; staminodes 5–10mm (¼–½in) wide; sepals obtuse.
Identify as **C. pedunculata** Sims.

6. Flowers pendent, reddish-purple, 10–14cm (4–5½in) long; leaves often lanuginose below.
Identify as **C. iridiflora** Ruiz & Pav.
or
6. Flowers erect. **Go to 7.**

7. Leaves glaucous, narrowly ovate to narrowly elliptic, base and apex very gradually narrowed; flowers generally yellow; rhizomes long-creeping.
Identify as **C. glauca** L.
or
7. Leaves not glaucous, generally ovate to elliptic and with an acute to acuminate apex; flowers never purely yellow, but with all kinds of colours between red and yellow; rhizomes short, tuberous. **Go to 8.**

8. Floral bracts persistent. **Go to 9.**
or
8. Floral bracts caducous. **Go to 10.**

9. Pedicels smooth, 2–10mm (¹⁄₁₆–½in) long, to 1.5cm (⅝in) in fruit; lower side of leaves smooth.
Identify as **C. indica** L.
or
9. Pedicels densely tuberculate just below the ovary, 5–10mm (¼–½in) long, to 2cm (¾in) in fruit; lower side of leaves more or less lanuginose.
Identify as **C. bangii** Kraenzl.

10. Pedicels 5mm (¼in) long, to 1cm (½in) in fruit; flowers orange, 5–7.5cm (2–3in) long, floral tube curved; seeds narrowly ellipsoid.
Identify as **C. jaegeriana** Urb.
or
10. Pedicels 0.5–3cm (¼–1½in) long, to 4.5cm (1¾in) in fruit; flowers orange-red, 5.5–9cm (2¼–3½in) long, floral tube not curved; seeds subglobose.
Identify as **C. tuerckheimii** Kraenzl.

variations of this canna suggest that it has been propagated on many occasions by seed, resulting in variability and inconsistency of naming.

C. 'Lanuginosa' This has yellowish-red flowers and grows to 90cm–1.2m (3–4ft). Native of Brazil and Peru.

C. 'Latifolia' One of the tallest-growing, often reaching more than 4m (14ft) in a season. Leaves are 90cm (3ft) long and up to 20cm (8in) wide. Red flowers.

C. 'Limbata' This has greenish-yellow flowers. A native of Brazil, it was introduced in 1818 and grows to 1.2m (4ft).

C. 'Lutea' Growing to 90cm (3ft) in height, this has pale yellowish-white flowers. Native to tropical and subtropical America.

C. 'Musifolia' (syn. C. 'Musaefolia') Immense dark green leaves with red veining and red stems make this an incredible foliage plant. It is very shy flowering and does not normally bloom under British conditions. However, in warm climates with long growing seasons, it may eventually produce small red flowers. It is extremely vigorous and will reach up to 4m (14ft) in a warm climate.

Botanists seem to be unable to clarify the nomenclature of this canna or even to decide whether it is a species or a hybrid, although the latter seems more likely. William Robinson refers to it in his *Subtropical Gardening* and says it was introduced by M. Année to France from Peru in 1858. It was originally listed in the Botanical Cabinet as C. *exelsa*. (If the plant we now grow is the same, under rules of botanical precedence, we should probably be using this name, although for horticultural purposes, 'C. *musifolia*' is very widely known.) There is little information to verify the origins of this plant but it seems to be well established in use and name by the 1870s. *Seventy Five Popular Flowers and How to Cultivate them*, published in 1870, refers to 'C. *musaefolia*' with large green leaves and red flowers. *Every Woman HER OWN Flower Gardener – A Handy Manual of Gardening for Ladies* 1871, also refers to the species and its 'large and handsome foliage'. Neither references speak of the stature of the plant, which is surely one of its main features.

C. 'Patens' See C. *indica*.

C. 'Speciosa' This has pale purple flowers and grows to 1.8m (6ft) in height. It was introduced from India and the East Indies in 1820.

C. 'Warszewiczii' This striking plant has green leaves, black stems and dark leaf veins, and produces small bright cherry-red flowers. It is quite compact, growing to no more than 90cm (3ft). One of the most attractive of the small-flowered cannas, it looks especially good planted with *Dahlia* 'Bishop of Llandaff'. Introduced from Costa Rica, Brazil in 1849, it was a key plant in the early breeding programmes and is probably the source of the purple leaves in the modern hybrids.

6

AN A–Z OF CANNAS

It has been estimated that several thousand cannas have been developed, offered for sale and grown since the nineteenth century. Many of these are now lost to cultivation. This section lists all the generally grown garden forms of canna and is based on plants that either I have grown or observed myself or are clearly identified in printed information. All those listed are thought to be available in cultivation. There are many others, both new and old, in collections and nurseries throughout the world.

Comments on availability can only be correct at the time of writing. However, it is obvious that even a new cultivar, if available from a commercial nursery and grown in thousands, is likely to be spread around more quickly than an individual plant seen in a private collection. In the British Isles, the *RHS Plant Finder* is the best source for locating different plants and there are equivalents of this book in other countries.

Although much of this information has been prepared from the study of living plants, the use of books and catalogues has been invaluable, especially in obtaining details on the older cultivars. However, readers should note that some information, such as the colour descriptions, will always be subjective.

One of the sources of information is the canna section of The International Checklist for Hyacinths and Miscellaneous Bulbs held by the Royal General Bulb Growers Association. This lists many cannas together with synonyms, descriptions, raiser's names and dates of introduction. In theory, this is a very valuable document and with older cultivars it is just that. However,

Dating from 1920, 'Assaut' is probably one of the most commonly grown red cultivars.

the registration is very out of date. Cannas sadly do not have a high commercial value, in comparison with say tulips or dahlias. The time spent on the registration reflects this! There are currently moves to place the responsibility for cannas to a more active authority and no doubt the imminent canna trial planned by the RHS will be very important in overhauling this registration.

C. × generalis L. H. Bailey

Cultivated plants, to 2m (6ft) tall. Leaves green or reddish-brown. Flowers erect, red, orange or yellow, often with spots or stripes of another colour, large and showy, 11–13cm (4½–5in) long, composed of 8 or more coloured parts; petals reflexed or not; staminodes 3 or more, to 5.5cm (2¼in) wide. Cultivated all over the tropics and many temperate areas.

This is the species into which all the modern hybrid cannas should be placed. For practical horticultural purposes, however, the specific name is rarely used. For example, C. × *generalis* 'King Humbert' is usually known as C. 'King Humbert'.

The taxonomist Bailey distinguished C. × *generalis* as having flowers to 10cm (4in) in diameter, not tubular at base, with petals not reflexed, staminodes and lip erect or spreading. This included, primarily, the Crozy or French-style cannas, most of which are diploid and fertile. He distinguished a second group, C. × *orchioides*, as having very large flowers, tubular at base and petals reflexed, usually splashed and mottled, and three broad and wavy staminodes exceeded by the lip. This latter group were the Italian or orchid-flowered cannas, such as 'Italia', many of which are triploid and sterile. With breeding, the distinction has become blurred and both groups are now lumped together as *C. × generalis*.

HEIGHT

The performance of cannas varies considerably according to many variable factors, all of which may inhibit or encourage growth. Under good growing conditions, with a fertile soil, abundant moisture and a long, warm growing season, the ultimate height will be considerably more than under more restrictive conditions. Growers in near-tropical conditions question whether there is any such thing as a 'dwarf' canna.

In the following descriptions, cannas are broadly grouped as short (S) up to 45cm (18in), medium (M) 45cm to 1.5m (18in to 5ft), and tall (T) more than 1.5m (5ft), according to their likely performance under an average temperate European summer. Such a grouping can only be a generalization but heights are likely to be within these ranges.

TERMINOLOGY

Throughout these descriptions, I have used 'petals' to describe the prominent floral characters. Technically, these are staminodes (p.28) but this term seems pedantic for general usage. The 'lip' is the larger 'petal' (staminode) that often protrudes at the base of the flower. In referring to the 'throat', I am using a non-technical term to allude to the tube-like centre of the flower, formed from the combined bases of the petals.

VARIEGATED CANNAS

Among the variegated cannas there are many synonyms, which include names based on cities. There is some general agreement among canna growers that, for simplicity, these names should take precedence over the others. Therefore we have 'Bankok', 'Durban', 'Kansas City', 'Pretoria' and 'Stuttgart'. The only widely grown variegated canna that does not have a city name is 'Pink Sunburst'.

'Adam's Orange' (M) This cultivar has medium-sized, yellow-orange flowers with overall reddish flush. The petals are neatly fanned and delicately frilled. Leaves are pointed and green.

'African Scarlet Speckle' (M) Although I have only seen it in one collection, this cultivar is distinctive enough to merit a place in this list. The massive heads of blooms are composed of loose, open flowers reminiscent of lilies. The colouring is a rich buttercup-yellow heavily overlaid with red speckles that unite into bold red blotches at the end of the petals and especially on the lip. Petals are slightly spooned and recurved. Green foliage provides a fine setting for the flowers. The origin of this cultivar is unknown.

'Aida' See Grand Opera Series.

'Alberich' (S) The flowers of this lovely old cultivar are soft pinkish, shading to orange and salmon, with some yellow feathering. Individual flowers are large and the petals wide, giving a very full shape. It is quite compact but produces sturdy, vigorous growth. The leaves are green with the added bonus of red stems, making the foliage particularly attractive. It was raised by Wilhelm Pfitzer in 1949.

'Aloha' (S) This recent cultivar has dark orange-red flowers with yellow markings, set off by greyish-green leaves with dark margins. It was raised in Longwood Gardens from a cross with 'Lanape', and it first flowered in 1990. It is a good example of a modern dwarf canna.

'Ambassador' (T) The brown leaves of this cultivar act as a fitting setting for the deep fiery-red flowers. Overall it is very similar, if not identical, to 'Black Knight'. Although separately registered in the 'International Checklist', there is no date or raiser information. Note the spelling.

'Ambassadour' (M) This impressive cultivar is truly eye-catching with its large, creamy-white, gladiolus-like flowers, the centre of each having a darker orange hue. On the second day, the flowers fade to pure ivory and it is, therefore, classed as one of the so-called whites. The leaves are large, paddle-like and slightly glaucous. The spelling of this and the previous cultivar often causes confusion.

'Ambrosia' (M) A compact cultivar with a fusion of salmon, orange and pink in the large flowers. The foliage is green. Available only from a few specialist nurseries in the USA and New Zealand.

'**America**' (M) This handsome old cultivar has intense scarlet flowers. The petals are long, thin and reflexed giving the bloom a very open, blowsy appearance. The leaves are a dark purplish-green with pronounced darker veins. There is an attractive white farina on the stems, which contrasts well with the deep red flowers. Raised by C. Sprenger in 1893, it is very similar to 'Black Knight' and 'Ambassador'.

'**Angel Pink**' (M) The overall effect is dusky pink; individual flowers are predominantly pink but close inspection reveals that each petal is a rich clotted-cream colour within the funnel, overlaid with heavy pink spots. These unite to form the pink body of the petal. The undersides of the petals are a tantalizing mix of pink and cream. This well-behaved cultivar is self-cleaning and compact with green foliage. Raised by Kent Kelly.

'**Anthony de Crozy**' (syn. 'Madame Crozy') (S) Offered by Podgora Gardens in New Zealand, this cultivar seems to be very similar, if not identical, to 'Lucifer' in cultivation. It produces a compact plant with narrowish leaves. The flowers are upright and medium-sized in red with a clear yellow margin. The name is of interest in that, if genuine, it was one of the first of Crozy's introductions in the nineteenth century. The plant does fit the early descriptions but there are, of course, no photographs for close comparison.

'**Aphrodite**' (M) Large, dusky pink flowers are produced over green foliage, which is tinted bronze when young. It has the added attraction of red stems and central leaf veins. Current stock is said to have been raised by van Klaveren. The original was raised by P. Schmid and fits the same description.

'**Apricot Dream**' (M) Compact plants are topped with a mass of buff-salmon blooms. Each flower has eye-catching touches of gold and deep pink within the centre. This cultivar is very free-flowering and also conveniently self-cleaning. Leaves are a greyish green. Another modern cultivar from Kent Kelly.

'**Apricot Frost**' (M) This prolific grower produces masses of large, salmon-pink flowers. The foliage is green.

'**Apricot Ice**' (M) Pure soft pale peach flowers over clean green leaves. It is generally self-cleaning and was raised by Kent Kelly.

'**Aranályom**' (M) This excellent cultivar produces luminous orange flowers with slightly darker stippling and yellow spots in throat. There are very fine yellow edges to the petals, which are reflexed and slightly rippled. This canna has green leaves and a good stocky habit of growth and was raised in Hungary in 1959.

'**Aristote**' (S) The flower colour of this cultivar is a silvery pink, appearing quite dark in the shade but glistening almost white in the sun. The petals are slightly cupped and the leaves are green. Available from Pierre Turc in France.

'**Assaut**' (syn. 'Vorwärts') (T) This handsome old cultivar has large, dark imperial-red flowers and dark bluish leaves with bronze veins. It was raised by Vilmorin-Andrieux in 1920 and stocks are still very vigorous. It is readily available and is the commonest red and bronze available in the British Isles and probably elsewhere. (It also seems to be identical to 'Hercule', 'Vainquer' and 'Lafayette'.) Flowers are softer scarlet-red than 'Black Knight' and less reflexed and shaggy.

'**Australia**' (T) The flowers of this splendid cultivar are large and a pearly salmon. However, the main feature is its brilliant burnished chestnut-brown leaves: it is probably the best tall, dark-leaved canna to date. Sadly, it is difficult to cultivate and likes to be kept growing throughout the winter, rather than being allowed to go dormant. It produces very few new divisions each year so plants are always expensive and in short supply.

The name is confusing as the 'International Checklist' describes 'Australia' as a yellow-flowered cultivar raised in 1906. That form seems to have been lost and the name is now widely used for this later cultivar, which seems to have originated from Podgora Gardens in New Zealand. Sonja Mrsich, the current owner, believes her parents acquired it from an unrecorded source. It can be dated as pre-1967 as it appears in pre-decimal currency lists, but its origins are unknown.

'**Autumn Gold**' (T) Although I have only seen this in one USA collection, it is a distinct cultivar. The tall

The true 'Black Knight' is one of the darkest red cannas in existence.

habit and greyish-green, lance-shaped leaves would suggest that it has C. *glauca* in its parentage. The flowers are medium-sized and quite upright, with narrow petals. The overall colour is cream with a touch of pink, accentuated by a curling pink lip and a prominent pink stigma. The effect is quite elegant. If it has C. *glauca* in its parentage, it is likely that this would perform as a water canna. It was introduced by Johnny Johnson in the late 1990s.

'Bankok' (syn. 'Striped Beauty', 'Christ's Light', 'King of Siam', 'Nirvana', 'Minerva') (M) This poor plant must suffer from an identity crisis! As well as all its other names, it is sometimes sold as C. *indica* var, which is definitely incorrect. It has green leaves with white splashes along veins which qualifies it for inclusion in the list of variegated cannas. Both good, clearly marked stocks as well as poor ones are available. Whether or not the foliage is of value, it has handsome bright yellow blooms with a white stripe on the petals producing the overall effect of a white cross in the flower. There is also a seductive mahogany throat.

One of the oldest of the variegated cannas, it was in cultivation by 1923 and is said to have originated from Thailand. It is readily available, but difficult to overwinter as it makes very small rhizomes and so it needs careful storage.

'Beatrix' (M) This compact cultivar has large flowers in a soft salmon. The leaves are green. Available in New Zealand.

'Begonia' (M) An American cultivar with creamy-white flowers and green leaves.

'Bengal Tiger' See 'Pretoria'.

'Black Knight' (syn. 'Black Velvet', possibly also a synonym for 'Ambassador') (T) 'Black Knight' is the name widely used in the British Isles for a cultivar with large, floppy, deep crimson flowers that have reflexed petals. The name also appears in Indian lists but is not registered. The stems bear an attractive contrasting white farina and the leaves are a bluish-purple. It is readily available, but stocks are often not true to type.

'Black Velvet' See 'Black Knight'.

'Bonfire' (M) The glowing orange-red flowers of this cultivar are medium-sized with frilly, reflexed petals. There is a splash of yellow on the lip and in the throat. The leaves are green. Readily available.

'Bonnezeaux' (M) The flowers of this cultivar are very shapely and elongated, with crinkly petals. They are a watery primrose-yellow that glistens in the sun. The foliage is green. It grows well in a planter. Available from Pierre Turc in France.

'Brandywine' (S) Flowers are orange-red with yellow centres and burnished gold on the lip. The green leaves have dark margins. It was raised by Longwood Gardens and first flowered in 1984. (This name was also used for a cultivar described in Henderson's 1909 catalogue as having bronze leaves and red flowers, dappled crimson and edged yellow. It is believed that this earlier cultivar is no longer available.)

'Brenda Elaine' (M) Another cultivar that I observed in a private collection. It has exquisite flowers of a clear shell-pink with touches of yellow in the throat. The petals are large and slightly waved giving a sophisticated effect. The leaves are large, shiny and green. This was introduced by Johnny Johnson in the 1990s and named after his wife.

'Brighton Orange' (M) This one has delicate, iris-like, soft orange flowers. The petals are quite narrow with a distinct notched tip. There is a touch of yellow in the throat and the petals are overlaid with slightly darker orange spots. It is compact and has narrow, bronze leaves. Similar to 'Verdi' but distinct. Originated from Brighton Parks Department in England.

'Brilliant' (S) Small, cherry-red, open-petalled flowers are very similar to 'Strasbourg'. It produces a compact plant with green leaves. Originally raised by A. Crozy although the date is not registered.

'Butterscotch' (M) Intense bright yellow flowers are borne over green foliage. Conveniently self-cleaning. Probably only available in the USA.

'Cabalero'® (S) This lovely true dwarf cultivar has a sturdy habit and green foliage. The flowers are in nicely rounded heads. Each individual flower is like a flattened trumpet with petals that do not quite overlap. The basic colour is clear buttercup-yellow with dainty red spotting. One of the creations of Ernest Turc.

'Caliente' (M) Large flowers with long petals in a bright, clear red. It has large, bronze leaves.

'Carnaval'® (M) This is a new introduction from Ernest Turc. Flowers are bright tangerine orange with a lighter golden edge and overall stippling of gold. The foliage is green. (The name is also registered to a salmon-pink Vilmorin-Andrieux introduction of 1911. Another example of the confusion in canna naming.)

'Brandywine' is a lovely new cultivar, raised by Longwood Gardens in the USA.

'Carousel' (M) An interesting new canna from Herb Kelly. 'Carousel' has multiple colours in each individual flower, opening soft pastel orange with occasional yellow streaks, turning pink with white streaks as the flower ages. A flower stalk will have the entire range of colours as the newer flowers emerge within the older flowers. Available from a few nurseries in the USA.

'Centenaire de Rozain-Boucharlat' (M) This splendid cultivar produces rich cerise-pink, gladiolus-like flowers. Green leaves with a fine dark margin. Early-flowering, of compact habit and very floriferous. This old cultivar was originally raised by A. Crozy, probably around 1925. It has been offered in Britain recently as 'Melanie'. Available in the British Isles and France.

'Centurion' (T) A tall cultivar with large, tangerine-orange flowers and green foliage. Raised by Ernest Turc in France.

PLATE IV
CANNA FLOWER SHAPES

'Brilliant'
(open-petalled)

'President'
(gladiolus-flowered)

'Eric Neubert' (iris-flowered)

'General Eisenhower'
(orchid-flowered)

'Wintzer's Colossal'
(large-flowered)

'Cerise Davenport'
(small-flowered)

'Lafayette' (reflexed flower)

'Marie Nagel'
(butterfly-flowered)

'Louis Cottin'
(trumpet-shaped)

'Puck' (frilled flower)

'City of Portland'
(typical raceme)

'Alberich'
(full-petalled)

All flowers are shown at approximately half lifesize

The rich burgundy foliage of 'Champigny' is a faultless setting for its cerise-pink flowers.

'**Cerase**' (M) Although not producing a mass of flowers, the effect of this cultivar is superb. The overall colour is sharp raspberry-pink but the centre is a contrasting white. The display is set off by green leaves. Probably as yet only available in the USA.

'**Cerise Davenport**' (M) These small flowers are curiously shrimp-like in shape and salmon-pink. The foliage is green and it is a strong-growing but compact cultivar. Probably only available in Britain.

'**C. F. Cole**' (S) This cultivar has soft lemon-yellow flowers, heavily spotted with large, soft pink dots. It bears green foliage. Probably only available from specialist nurseries.

'**Champigny**' (M) This pretty cultivar is attractive as a quite young plant with its very luxuriant, deep burgundy foliage. This is quickly topped with numerous medium-sized, bright cerise flowers. Although the

'Champion' freely produces its large salmon-pink flowers and is easy to grow.

flower heads are not large, flowering is early and continuous. It is self-cleaning. A recent introduction from Pierre Turc.

'**Champion**' (M) Large, soft salmon-pink flowers overlaid with streaks of darker almost red colouring and flushes of gold in the throat. It has light bronze foliage. Raised by Ernest Turc and available in Britain and France.

'**Cheerfulness**' (M) Although not huge, the shapely flowers are very effective in vivid russet-orange with a pale creamy centre. Each petal is also rimed with an irregular yellow margin. Petals are slightly rippled and twisted in an irregular way giving an attractive result. The foliage is green and the origin is unknown.

'**Cherry Red**' See 'Pfitzer's Cherry Red'.

'**Chesapeake**' (M) A vigorous cultivar producing pale yellow flowers, fading to creamy-white. The tidy grey-

green foliage makes a first-rate foil for the flowers. It was raised by Longwood Gardens and first flowered in 1980.

'China Doll' (M) Masses of deep raspberry-pink flowers are produced throughout the season by this reliable cultivar. It is suitably self-cleaning with green foliage. Raised by Kent Kelly. One of my abiding memories of my trip to the USA in 2000 will be sitting beside a field of this cultivar in the setting sun!

'China Lady' (M) This is another Kent Kelly introduction with coral-pink flowers and green leaves.

'China Lass' (M) Yet another in the Kelly series, this time with huge, coral-pink flowers over green foliage.

'Chinese Coral' (T) This opulent cultivar has large, rich salmon-pink, gladiolus-like flowers. The plant is of great stature with substantial, broad and slightly glaucous leaves. Raised by P. Schmid. This is not the same as 'Pfitzer's Chinese Coral', which is more compact and a brighter pink. Inevitably there is some confusion here, as many stocks exist under this name.

'City of Portland' (syn. 'Orchid') (M) This familiar cultivar gives rich salmon flowers with yellow flushing and a matching pencilled edge. The whole effect is quite bright and gaudy. It is utterly reliable and very generous in its quantity of flower. However, it is untidy as dead flowers do not fall. Although widely available, it is a brash, harsh colour and there are many better cannas available.

In Britain, it is widely grown as 'Orchid', which is also a registered name. 'City of Portland' was originally raised by Wintzer and described as a 'magnificent new variety' in 1916. The formal registration refers to jasper red flowers, but most stocks of this are a clear pink adding even further to the confusion. However, by 1921, Buist's catalogue describes it as 'bright rosy pink'.

'Cleopatra' (syn. 'Yellow Humbert', 'Spanish Emblem') (T) This curious cultivar is technically known as a periclinal chimera. The plant can produce large, yellow flowers with red spots or pure tomato-red flowers or even flowers bearing combinations of both colour-ways, sometimes even split down the centre of the petals. The foliage is generally green but occasional brown sectors appear. Sometimes shoots are produced that can be entirely green with yellow blooms. Likewise, sometimes there are entirely brown-leaved shoots and these always produce red flowers. This latter version can be stabilized and is known as 'Red Cleopatra'.

Overall the plant is unstable as it contains mixed genetic material within its tissues, which can give rise to any of the above combinations. Studying the shoots one can often observe small, purple streaks, showing the inclusion of the darker tissues which will give rise to dark leaves or red flowers. In India this cultivar is also known as 'Queen of Italy' and is said to have arisen as a chimera from 'King Humbert'. It was in existence at least by 1895. With such an unstable plant, there are inevitably both good and bad stocks. When making a purchase, it is wise to look for plants that have a good mix of bronze and green in the leaves. It is readily available throughout the world.

'Cleopatre' (M) An elegant cultivar with medium-sized, orange flowers with faint gently rippled, yellow edges. The petals are narrow giving a delicate butterfly-like effect. It has green foliage. This French cultivar is totally different to 'Cleopatra'.

'Cole's Pale Superba' (M) This splendid canna produces huge heads of large, flat, pale sulphur-apricot flowers, each with a golden centre. The buds are a darker apricot with a purple hue. When well grown, it is tall and vigorous with rich green foliage. It is lovely but difficult to obtain and there seem to be some poor weak, possibly virus-infected stocks in circulation.

'Colibri' (syn. 'Confetti') (M) More generally available under the synonym, this has pale yellow flowers, liberally spotted with pink dots. It was originally raised by G. Truffaut in 1966. The name is often used for any spotted, yellow canna and it is unknown whether the correct stock is still available.

'Colossal' See 'Wintzer's Colossal'.

'Conestoga' (M) A modern cultivar with large flowers in clear bright lemon-yellow, the petals being attractively fluted. The soft grey-green leaves form a dramatic background to the freely produced flowers. It was

The soft yellow flowers of 'Conestoga' are backed by subtle grey-green foliage.

raised by Longwood Gardens and originally flowered in 1979 but is as yet not widely available.

'Confetti' See 'Colibri'.

'Constitution' (M) The flowers of this exquisite cultivar are the palest of powder pink with large, overlapping petals with a slight 'nick' at the end. The centre warms to a mellow cream. All this is set off by muted pewter-bronze foliage. This is just the plant for those who complain that cannas are all brash and gaudy! It was raised by Longwood Gardens and first flowered in 1978. Not as yet widely available.

'Coq d'Or' Probably a synonym for 'Oiseau d'Or'.

'Corail' (M) This semi-dwarf plant has bright tomato-red flowers over purple foliage. Available from Ernest Turc in France.

'Corrida' (S) Another true dwarf cultivar that has brilliant red flowers over green foliage. Available from Ernest Turc in France.

'Corsica' See Island Series.

'Cote d'Or' (M) A traditional cultivar with chrome-yellow flowers highlighted with striking red pencilled markings in the throat. An upright plant with green foliage. Originated from Brighton Parks Department.

'Cream' This is probably the same as 'Ambassadour', although there is a 'Cream Beauty' registered.

'Crimson Beauty' (T) Plants of this are generally tall and bear medium-sized, dark red flowers with daintily reflexed petals. The green leaves have a fine dark rim. There is some doubt that the stock now available under this name is original as there are earlier references to it being a dwarf raised by Wilhelm Pfitzer; in the USA there are some stocks that fit this latter description.

'Cupid' (M) This semi-dwarf canna has light pink and lavender flowers and dark green foliage. Available from a few specialist nurseries in the USA and New Zealand.

'Declaration' (M) Another one of the Longwood Cannas raised in 1973. It has bright red flowers backed by alluring greyish-green leaves. The centre of the flowers has touches of gold and silvery-white. As yet not widely available.

'Delaware' (M) This compact cultivar has large flowers in a deep coral with a purplish hint and green leaves. Raised by Longwood Gardens and first flowered in 1972, but still not readily available.

'Délibáb' (S) The registration of this cultivar, raised in Hungary in 1966, describes a plant with burnt-orange flowers shaded red. It should be stocky with leathery, dull brown leaves and is one of very few dark-leaved short cannas. However, there are some very dubious stocks available under this name in almost any colour!

'Di Bartolo' (T) This tall cultivar has large, deep pink flowers, well presented above luxuriant purple foliage. It is available in Britain and from Pierre Turc in France.

'**Dolly Gay**' (M) Flowers are a solid tomato-red and shaped like a small cymbidium orchid. In the throat the colour breaks up into red blotches over cream and eventually becomes pure cream. Petals have a fine cream margin. Similar to 'Cheerfulness' but darker.

'**Dondo**' (M) This so-called white cultivar has large, smooth, cream flowers with fine purple dots. It has waxy green leaves and is very similar to 'Oiseau d'Or'.

'**Durban**' (syn. 'Tropicanna'™, 'Phasion') (M) The version generally available in Britain has psychedelic purple foliage with pink veins, fading to orange. To date, the most exotic and outrageously coloured canna in existence, it has large, vivid mandarin-orange flowers, similar to 'Wyoming', from which it is said to have derived. It is a vigorous grower and tillers well.

The 'Durban' Story

In 1993, I heard of a canna with brilliantly coloured foliage, named 'Durban', and immediately coveted it. Although I understood that the plant had originated from the city of Durban in South Africa, the only commercial sources seemed to be in the USA and were horrendously expensive. When a friend asked me if there was anything I wanted from South Africa, where he was going on holiday, I described 'Durban' to him. I was not optimistic that he, a non-gardener, would ever find this highly desirable plant, but to my astonishment a few weeks later a small package arrived. My friend had found the canna growing in a hedgerow on a nursery. The owner had been reluctant to dig it up, describing it as a weed. It grew, produced psychedelic leaves and huge, orange flowers, becoming an instant success.

In 1997 a cultivar named 'Phasion' was imported from the USA. This had been selected by Jan Potgeither in Bethal, South Africa and it would appear that this name is licensed under US Patents. 'Phasion' was subsequently renamed 'Tropicanna'™ and Plant Protected, which means the name cannot be used, nor the cultivar commercially propagated, without authority from Anthony Tesselaar, who owns the rights. I have grown all three cultivars, over several seasons, and can see no difference between them whatsoever.

The gaudy orange flowers of 'Durban' are an added bonus to the brilliant foliage.

To add to the confusion, there is also a red-flowered 'Durban' in the USA, which was imported, again from South Africa, by Gary Hammer of Desert to Jungle Nursery, in 1991. Although offered commercially by 1993, its initial high price of $100, prevented its wide distribution. It has inferior foliage but good-sized, soft red flowers and, although mediocre in comparison to the orange-flowered cultivar, is worth growing as a collector's plant. It seems that this red form preceded the orange one, being available in 1993, although it did not reach Britain until later. It is, therefore, possible that the name 'Durban' was erroneously applied to the better, orange form, when it was first introduced to Britain.

Although, theoretically, the acceptance of the names 'Phasion' or 'Tropicanna'™ could be made, this would cause considerable confusion in Britain. Also the many nurserymen who are legitimately selling 'Durban' would be loath to lose such a right by accepting a patented name. It is suggested that the two types are designated 'Orange Durban' and 'Red Durban'.

'**Effie Cole**' (M) Green leaves set off the dusky mid-pink flowers of this cultivar. Each of the wavy petals is

edged in lemon-yellow and the centre of the flower is a similar colour. I saw this lovely cultivar in the collection at Missouri Botanic Garden but it is otherwise unverified.

'Ehemanii' See *C. iridiflora* (p.57).

'Eileen Gale' (syn. 'Eileen Gallo') (T) Pale pewter-bronze foliage suitably sets off the very pale pink blooms of this cultivar. The habit is vigorous. Another seen on my visit to Missouri Botanic Garden but otherwise unverified.

'Elizabeth Hoss' (M) This cultivar bears massive red flowers with reflexed petals. The green leaves have thin red margins. The name is not verified but it is a lovely flower on a statuesque plant. Generally only in a few collections.

'Elma Cole' (M) Another cultivar from the prodigious Australian breeder Cole. This one has light clear yel-

low flowers and green foliage. Only available from specialist nurseries.

'Emblème' (T) This cultivar has vivid red flowers set-off perfectly by dark foliage. If current stock is accurate, it was originally raised in 1927 by H. Cayeaux, although it looks similar to many other reds available today. Mainly available in France.

'Empire' (M) A modern canna with red blooms borne over a very compact plant with green leaves. Raised by Kent Kelly.

'En Avant' (syn. 'Golden Bird') (M) This is a popular and easily grown cultivar. It has bright apple-green leaves and freely produced golden-yellow flowers that are beautifully sprinkled with red dots. This is one of the best of the spotted-flower cannas and is frequently admired. Raised by Vilmorin-Andrieux in 1914. It is readily available.

'Endeavour' (T) One of the water cannas raised at Longwood Gardens. It has soft raspberry-red, iris-like flowers with elongated petals. The leaves are narrow and have a glaucous sheen, which demonstrates its derivation from *C. glauca*. The plant is very tall and slender and the overall effect is quite charming. It can be grown as a waterside plant or in a border with other cannas. It was introduced in 1977.

'Erebus' (M) Another water canna from Longwood Gardens, this cultivar has soft pale salmon, iris-like flowers. It is shorter and more compact than 'Endeavour' but also has glaucous foliage.

'Eric Neubert' (syn. 'E. Neubert') (M) A flamboyant canna bearing medium-sized, erect, flame-coloured flowers with a touch of yellow in the throat. It is an upright plant with narrow, pale bronze leaves. It is very similar to 'Verdi' but, when compared at close quarters, is distinct.

'Etoile du Feu' (M) This attractive canna cultivar produces shapely, tomato-red blooms with yellow

'En Avant' is among the best of the many red-spotted, yellow canna cultivars.

throats, making a very rich colour mix. Free flowering and with bronze foliage, it is often one of the first to flower.

'Eureka' (M) The flowers of this old cultivar open very pale primrose peppered with red dots and fade to ivory-white. Large, blue-green leaves. It was raised by Henry Dreer in 1918, although other records suggest that it was raised in 1950 by Wayside Gardens. It is sometimes classed as a 'white' canna. A fertile cultivar, it forms many seeds and it is likely that, over the years, the stock has become impure due to the influx of seedlings. This may explain why many stocks are disappointing.

'Evening Star' Although the name is registered, current stocks seem to be identical to 'Perkeo'.

'Extase' (M) This lovely French cultivar has very full compact heads of large flowers with wavy petals. It is an exquisite shade of pale salmon-pink with slightly ruffled petals giving an exquisite overall effect. It is a stocky, well-behaved plant with slightly glaucous green leaves. Quite widely available.

'Fatamorgana' Although this name is registered, current stocks seem to be identical to 'Perkeo'.

'Favourite' (M) This cultivar has large, carmine-pink flowers. It makes a stocky plant with green foliage. The 'International Checklist' suggests it was raised by P. Schmid in 1962.

'Felix Ragout' (M) The large, golden-yellow, funnel-shaped flowers of this cultivar make it quite distinct. They are borne in large, well-rounded heads over green foliage. Very similar to and possibly the same as 'King City Gold', it is widely available.

'Feuerzauber' (syn. 'Fire Magic', 'Feu Magique') (M) This classic old cultivar has striking orange-scarlet flowers in an irregular trumpet shape. The shapely heads are set off by soft brown leaves. It was raised by Wilhelm Pfitzer in 1922 but, inevitably, the name has been changed according to the country selling it.

'Firebird' (M) A well-known name applied to a cultivar with fiery crimson flowers and simple green foliage.

Dating back to 1893, 'Florence Vaughan' (p.76) can still be considered as a quite spectacular cultivar.

The Storrs and Harrison Co of Painesville Ohio, 1916, described it in glowing terms, explaining that 'this variety has so captivated visitors who have seen it in bloom, it has been hard for propagators to acquire a proper amount of stock to launch it on the market'.

'Fireside' (M) A compact, stocky plant with large, paddle-shaped, slightly glaucous leaves. It has huge, gladiolus-like, scarlet-red flowers with a small, yellow throat. It is a very good, reliable grower. Although it is similar to 'President', it is without the fine yellow margin. The cultivar is readily available in Britain, although the name does not seem to be in common usage elsewhere.

'Flameché' (S) This diminutive cultivar grows to only about 40cm (15in) making it one of the shortest of all cannas. It is very free flowering, covering itself with medium-sized, orange blooms. Available from Pierre Turc in France.

'**Florence Vaughan**' (T) Another lovely old Victorian cultivar that has stood the test of time. It has large, frilled, orchid-shaped flowers in lemon-yellow marked with orange blotching and spotting.

The name is sometimes used for other, inferior, yellows such as 'King Midas'. To add to the confusion, it is occasionally sold in the USA as 'Yellow Humbert', which is also incorrect. The 'International Checklist' gives the raiser as A. Crozy and the date of registration as 1893. However, Vaughan's of Chicago refer to it in their catalogue as having been introduced by them in 1892. Whatever its background, it is a lovely cultivar.

'**Fournaise**' (M) This one has large, scarlet, gladiolus-like flowers. It has a compact habit and the foliage is green. A modern cultivar, available from Pierre Turc in France, it seems to be very similar to 'President' and 'Fireside'.

'**Francis Berti**' See 'Perkeo'.

'**Franklin**' (M) The large flowers of this cultivar range from yellow through orange to red. It has dark green

leaves, flushed purple with dark margins. It was raised by Longwood Gardens and originally flowered in 1984. Not as yet widely available.

'**Frau Gattenburg**' (syn. 'Frau Gartenburg') (T) This tall, green-leaved cultivar bears elegant curved heads of lemon-yellow flowers, which have a heavy contrasting red centre. Another cultivar I saw at Missouri Botanic Garden.

'**Freedom**' (M) Yet another cultivar raised by Longwood Gardens. The flowers are yellow, flushed reddish-orange. Compact plants bear medium green leaves with transparent margins. Not as yet widely available.

'**French Plum**' (T) Large, rose-pink flowers with wide overlapping petals giving a very full effect. Green leaves. Available from some European nurseries.

'**Furst Weid**' (M) This canna has intense red flowers of a delicate open shape with some yellow in the throat. It has nicely formed heads with a spire-like stem of buds covered in white farina. The foliage is green.

Futurity Series This series has been recently developed by Kent Kelly of the Quality Gladiolus Nursery. The plants perform exceedingly well under hot USA summers. As yet very few are available in Britain, where they are untried, although they should have good potential. All have been well trialled in the USA and have a 'high performance' specification, being of a good habit and all having a degree of self-cleaning. (See also Liberty™ Series, p.86.)

'**Pink Futurity**' (syn. 'Liberty™ Pink') (S) This has huge blooms with pure soft pink flowers over rich burgundy foliage. It is self-cleaning.

'**Red Futurity**' (S) This superlative cultivar has intense crimson flowers and rich 'dark chocolate' foliage. It is the latest in the series. The foliage colour is excellent and possibly darker than the renowned 'Australia' but with a compact habit. It is self-cleaning.

'**Rose Futurity**' (syn. 'Liberty™ Coral Rose') (S) Similar to 'Pink Futurity' but deep rose-pink with burgundy foliage.

The lush flowerheads of 'Gaiety' are sometimes so heavy that they trail downwards.

Despite perhaps humble origins, 'Giant Red' is good for a background plant or as a quick-filler.

'**Yellow Futurity**' (syn. 'Liberty™ Sun') (S) This canna has bright yellow flowers with soft red spots. It is quite free flowering and totally self-cleaning. The foliage is green.

'**Gaiety**' (syn. 'Color Clown') (M) It is surprising that this lovely cultivar is not more widely grown. It bears huge, open flowers reminiscent of a parrot tulip. Bright red blends into pure yellow in the centre, through massed blotches and streaks. It has green foliage. Not new, but not yet readily available.

'**General Eisenhower**' (M) Stocks of this cultivar are widely grown in Britain, although the name is not verified. It has hefty, ornate, mandarin-orange flowers. Even when not in flower, the huge, waxy, burgundy leaves make a considerable statement.

'**Giant Red**' (T) This oldie has smallish, red-orange flowers over vigorous, lush foliage. It is a good background plant or quick filler. The name is doubtful and very similar types are sold under various non-registered names. All are dismissively referred to as 'outhouse cannas' in the USA.

'**Gladiflora**' (T) If the stock is true, this old canna dates to pre-1884. It has enormous pink flowers, the spikes being large and each flower very full with substantial overlapping petals. It is reputed to be similar to 'French Plum'.

'**Glowing Embers**' (M) On this canna, deep green leaves are topped with primrose-yellow flowers, each petal embellished with bold red brush strokes. The name is not verified.

'**Gnom**' (S) This is one of the older-style dwarf cannas. It is very compact, with large, pale salmon flowers.

PLATE V

YELLOW-FLOWERED CANNAS

'En Avant'

'Sémaphore'

'Golden Girl'

'Heinrich Seidel'

'Elma Cole'

'Ambassadour'

'C. F. Cole'

All flowers are shown at approximately half lifesize

'Florence Vaughan'

'King City Gold'

C. glauca

'Conestoga'

'Puck'

'Richard Wallace'

The short stature of 'Golden Girl' makes it admirably suitable for patio planters.

However, it tends to hide the flowers in the foliage, a feature that has been bred out of the modern dwarfs. Raised by Wilhelm Pfitzer in 1949.

'Golden Girl' (S) Strong yellow flowers covered in tiny, red dots make a bold display on this cultivar. It is early- and continuous-flowering, and its compact habit makes it suitable for planters.

'Gran Canaria' See Island Series.

'Grand Duc' (M) The simple orange flowers are iris-like and are produced above bronze foliage. It is rather like 'Verdi'. Available in Britain and France.

'Grande' (T) This one is a must for those that like gigantic foliage or are creating an exotic garden. The huge, wavy, green leaves are finely rimmed with maroon and matched by dark ribs and stems.

For the lush foliage effect, this is one of the best! In most seasons it will probably reach at least 2.4m (8ft) and so should be used as a specimen plant or for the back of the border. It occasionally rewards the patient

gardener with small, red-orange flowers at the end of the year, although it would not normally be grown for its floral effect. It is probably a variant of 'Musifolia' (p.60) and undoubtedly better and easier to grow. In particular, it makes more substantial rhizomes, which are easier to overwinter.

Grand Opera Series This series was originally developed by Howard and Smith Nursery of Los Angeles, California in the 1930s. Wayside Gardens later purchased the series and added their own 'Rosenkavalier'. All cultivars have large flowers in pastel shades, green foliage and are quite tall. The whole of this range can be recommended for those that do not like the more ostentatious cannas. Sadly, they are not widely available, especially in Britain and there are many cannas sold, erroneously labelled with these names.

'Aida' (T) This has large, gladiolus-type flowers in a warm salmon-rose fading to pale salmon. The petals are lightly frilled. Like its musical namesake, it can be quite spectacular when well staged.

'La Bohème' (M) The large flowers are very frilly and ruffled. Soft peach tints are overlaid with pearl and subtle hints of yellow in the throat. This is really the Prima Donna of this theatrical series!

'La Traviata' (M) The darkest of this series, this has large flowers in a rich rose deepening to wine (the colour of Violetta's boudoir?). It is slightly yellow in the throat. The edges of the petals are primly frilly.

'Madame Butterfly' (M) This is the palest of the series with large, gladiolus-like flowers in ivory, overlaid with shell-pink. (The innocent young 'Butterfly'?) It has a curious furled, rounded flower shape with some similarity to a camellia.

'Mignon' (T) This is probably the brightest of this sophisticated group with vibrant orange-pink flowers. The flowers have elaborately pleated petals giving a very opulent effect. Broad foliage.

'Rigoletto' (M) Acclaimed in the past as the 'finest yellow canna grown'. It has huge, frilly, canary-yellow blooms – show stoppers.

'Rosenkavalier' (M) The name meaning 'The Knight of the Rose' aptly describes this bold cultivar with large, pink flowers.

The lush foliage and exuberant growth of 'Grande' make it an ideal subject for an exotic border.

'Halloween' (M) This is an unusual cultivar with delicate butterfly-like flowers. It has three petals in the top half of the bloom and just a small, twisted lip in the lower half. The colour is primarily a warm ivory-white with hints of pink but the throat is a deep cherry-red. Although not a large flower, the effect is quite superb. The foliage is green and flower buds have a purplish hue. It is not common but I observed it in private collections in the USA. It is thought to have been introduced by Mrs Sarver (p.21).

'Harvest Gold' (M) Another with bright yellow flowers with paler spots. The flower is quite large and the overlapping, slightly crinkled petals give a full effect. It has green leaves.

'Harvest Yellow' (M) This distinct canna has small, yellow flowers with tiny red dots. The overriding effect is quite delicate. It is worth growing in a collection but is not a stunner.

'Heinrich Seidel' (T) When in bloom, this cultivar is quite striking – the bright canary-yellow flowers have deep orange centres and delicate feathering – however, it can be disappointing due to the lateness of the flowering. The apple-green foliage is clean and attractive. Raised by Dammann and Veitch before 1898. It is not widely available.

'Hercule' (syn. 'Herculus') (T) The hefty scarlet flowers and purple foliage of this cultivar are very similar to 'Assaut', 'Vainquer' and 'Lafayette'. In simple garden comparisons, it is impossible to distinguish them although all names, except 'Vainquer', are registered. Available particularly in France.

'Horn' (M) This is quite a short cultivar with cabbage-green leaves. It has large, gladiolus-like, soft salmon-pink flowers with creamy centres, held well above foliage.

'Hungaria' (M) The large, rose-pink blooms of this cultivar are edged with cream. The leaves are green. It was raised by Árpád Mühle.

'H. W. Cole' (M) This Australian cultivar has beautiful glowing orange-red flowers with a coppery sheen, and green leaves. Although not readily available, it is well worth seeking out.

'Independence' (M) The large, lemon-yellow flowers are copiously produced. It has green leaves with transparent margins. This cultivar is shy at producing rhizomes, so is often difficult to obtain. It was raised by Longwood Gardens in 1977.

'Ingeborg' (M) An old cultivar with apricot-orange, iris-like flowers. The wavy, bronze foliage has an alluring waxy finish. Raised by Wilhelm Pfitzer in 1916.

'Intrigue' (T) This recent introduction from the USA is mainly grown for its lovely foliage. It has a slender habit with narrow, rich bronze foliage. The small, soft apricot-orange flowers are not unattractive but do not contribute a great amount to the impression. It is very tall so makes a good background or statement plant. It was raised by Herb Kelly.

'Isis' (S) Glaucous foliage shows off the delicate ivory-white flowers with pink centres. Compact habit. I raised this new cultivar. It has *C. glauca* in its parentage, so it is likely to be suitable for aquatic culture along with the other water cannas.

Island Series This is a group of four cannas, raised in the late 1990s by Takii of Japan. They are propagated by meristem culture and distributed as young plugs each spring for growing on by nurserymen; because of this they are very healthy and free of virus. They are early-flowering and can be programmed to flower in about ten weeks from potting. All are compact and have green foliage. The flowers are medium-sized, iris-like and freely produced. (Recent information suggests they may be removed from widespread commercial production because of problems with tissue culture.)
   'Corsica' (S) Soft apricot flowers.
   'Gran Canaria' (S) Pale primrose-yellow flowers, fading to near white.
   'Kreta' (S) Delicate orange-red flowers. The foliage of this one is quite narrow.
   'Madeira' (S) Deep pinkish-red flowers.

'Italia' (syn. 'Le Roi) (T) This splendid cultivar has monumental flowers like enormous cattleya orchids.

They are wavy petalled, bright yellow and heavily blotched and spotted with tomato-red. The lower petal is almost entirely red with a narrow yellow margin. This stately plant has enormous, waxy, glaucous-green leaves and is very vigorous and tall. It was raised by C. Sprenger in 1893 and is said to be a cross between 'Madame Crozy' and C. *flaccida*. This was the first of the 'new' orchid-flowering cannas and caused a sensation when it was first released. Not readily available.

'Italia' Rediscovered

I have often read mouth-watering descriptions of old cannas and wondered how such glorious plants have disappeared. In particular the description of 'Italia', a novelty for 1895, caught my attention. *The Gardeners' Chronicle* described it as having 'a beautiful golden, vermilion flower shaped like a giant cattleya orchid'. The characteristics of this plant were described in glowing detail over a number of pages. For several years, I searched for this plant, submitting its description to the 'Pink List', a register of plants thought to have been lost to cultivation. There was no response and I concluded that it seemed to have been totally lost. However, in the autumn of 1997, we received a small brown package from Peter Edgar, a fellow canna collector who travels the world. Inside was a canna root and a note that simply said 'from Madras Botanics'. October is a pessimistic time for cannas, and this one was too small to remain dormant, so I started it into growth and coaxed it through the winter. In spring it grew away vigorously producing huge, paddle-shaped, bluish leaves. When its first flower opened in early summer, it became evident that this was something special and unlike any other I had in the collection at the time. The flowers were larger than any canna I had ever seen. Using a quick measurement, it was impossible to span the flower between thumb and extended forefinger.

Over the following months I always had this huge flower in my mind as I scanned descriptions hoping to find a possible identification. I eventually recalled the accounts of 'Italia'. Comparisons of our new plant with the detailed descriptions given in nineteenth-century editions of *The Gardeners' Chronicle* fitted perfectly: 'The Canna Italia is a grand plant exceeding 6 feet in height, with Musa-like leaves and enormous spikes of brilliant red flowers bordered with yellow … The jury interpreting the general admiration and considering that nothing of the kind had been exhibited before, awarded Messrs Dammann and Co the Diploma of Honour.' Furthermore, black and white illustrations showed its flower markings corresponded with those on our flowers. It is difficult to know for certain if we have rediscovered 'Italia' but it seems likely that just over a hundred years after its debut, it has made a spectacular come-back!

'**Jasmine**' (S) This low-growing cultivar has very pale creamy-yellow flowers that are almost hidden by the foliage. Looks very similar to 'Puck' and may be the same. Seen on my visit to Missouri Botanic Gardens.

'**J. B. van der Schoot**' (M) Yet another canna with yellow flowers, striped and spotted dark red within. The petals are distinctly 'spooned', giving it some individuality. It is another old cultivar raised by Wilhelm Pfitzer in 1902.

'**Jivago**' (M) The large blooms of this canna are a deep clear orange with yellow in the throat. It was raised by Ernest Turc. Available in France and Britain.

'**Jolene**' (T) This one was possibly named after Jolene Snow of Horn Canna Farm. It is a tall-growing cultivar with green leaves. The golden-centred flowers are large and round with frilly, wavy petals in bright raspberry-red. I saw it in a private collection in the USA. I don't know if this name is verified, but this is a lovely, very 'growable' canna and should be more widely available.

'**Journey's End**' (syn. 'Fay's Orchid') (S) A widely grown canna with medium-sized, iris-like flowers in pale yellow, heavily spotted and overlaid with powder pink. The height seems to be variable. Although classed as short, it responds to generous conditions with vigorous growth and may reach 1.5m (5ft). It was raised by Patrick Malcolm and is readily available.

'**Kandy Apple**' (M) As well as starting to flower early, this cultivar continues to bloom freely throughout the season. The flowers are large and watermelon-red over green foliage. Another from Kent Kelly.

'**Kansas City**' (syn. 'Munchkin') (M) The green leaves of this cultivar are irregularly variegated with lemon-yellow and lime. It is a variable grower, which can look spectacular but because of its mutant nature often produces poorly variegated shoots that are very disappointing and may even look diseased. It has yellow flowers and was raised by J. Waddick. There is some debate as to whether 'Munchkin' is distinct as it is reputed to come from a different source. It also looks very similar to 'Aaron's Golden Ribbon'.

'Katha Rice' (M) This is another cultivar I saw in a private collection in the USA, but well worth seeking out. The flowers are a subtle shell-pink finished with a sheen to the petals. At the centre, this dissolves through pink spots on white to an almost pure white; the reverse of the petals is also an ivory-white. The foliage is green. Introduced by the TyTy Plantation.

'King City Gold' (M) The rounded heads of flowers on this cultivar are quite distinct. Individual flowers are iris-like and vivid sunflower-yellow with red dots, clearly pencilled in lines along the petals. It has green leaves and is very similar and possibly the same as 'Felix Ragout'.

'King Hakon' (M) This is a lovely cultivar with soft apricot flowers. The foliage is a very rich burnished bronze – one of the best brown-leaved types. The habit of growth is quite slender. It originated at Brighton Parks, but the name is not registered.

'King Humbert' (T) The name of this canna is probably one of the best known throughout the world and is used in the trade for numerous red-flowered cultivars with dark foliage. The original name for the 1902 cultivar raised by Sprenger is 'Roi Humbert', although this is confusing as the current cultivar offered under this name, by Turc et Fils, a major French canna producer, does not match the original descriptions.

The 1916 catalogue of the Storrs and Harrison Co describes 'King Humbert' as: 'The grandest canna ever offered. Large, heart-shaped leaves of purple madder brown over bronze, the dark ribs sharply defined, crowned with immense heads of orchid-like flowers. Individual petals are of the largest size; velvety orange-scarlet flecked carmine; rose tinted at the margin and base. A combination of leaf and blossom incomparably beautiful.' Flowers should be a rich orange-red. Many

'Königin Charlotte' has attracted attention ever since its introduction in 1892.

USA stocks are sold as 'Red King Humbert', which has a dark foliage and rich deep orange-red flowers. At this stage, it is impossible to tell which is the correct cultivar.

'King Midas' See 'Richard Wallace'.

'Königin Charlotte' (syn. 'Reine Charlotte', 'Queen Charlotte') (M) This lovely old canna was described in a 1902 catalogue as having 'enormous flower spikes, towering grandly above the foliage, bearing a beautiful bouquet of large flowers of perfect form, with petals of velvety blood red, banded with a border of canary yellow'. This is basically accurate but the flowers are medium-sized and iris-like. The plant is quite compact

'L'Aiglon' (M) A very ordinary canna with large, bright fiery-red flowers produced over huge, glaucous-green leaves. It bears a similarity to 'President' and does not seem to be distinct. It is available in France particularly.

'La Quintinie'® (S) This is another new introduction from Ernest Turc. The flowers are large and gently ruffled giving an opulent effect. The overall colour is a deep apricot that is overlaid with brushstrokes of light red, creating a dazzling light orange effect. The foliage is green but with a bronze sheen and purple veins.

'La Traviata' See Grand Opera Series.

'Lemon Yellow' (S) This tiny little canna is so small that it has been nicknamed 'the tea-cup canna' by Kent Kelly who raised it. Despite its diminutive size, it is prolific flowering, producing heads of medium-sized, lemon-yellow flowers clear of the foliage. It has clean grey-green leaves.

'Lenape' (M) Yet another of the Longwood cannas raised in 1984. This one has funnel-shaped flowers of bright golden-yellow heavily peppered with large, red spots. Petals are spooned. It has green leaves with transparent margins.

'L. G. Cole' (M) This unusual cultivar has large, sulphur-yellow flowers with an apricot blush broadly washed over the centre of the flower. It has green foliage. Only available from specialist nurseries.

'Liberation' (M) This lovely canna seems to have a whole series of colours within its large flowers. Overall it is a warm apricot but there is a pale candyfloss-pink feathering and darker orange within the throat. The older flowers fade to a paler tint, giving yet another colour-way. The buds and stems are a sallow purple covered in a white farina, which gives a soft, almost lavender colour, contrasting well with the flowers. It has plain, narrowish, green foliage. Raised in 1920 by Vilmorin-Andrieux and available from specialist nurseries, particularly in France.

'Liberté' (T) This look-alike canna has large, soft orange flowers and good rich purple foliage. The name

with apple-green leaves. It is very similar to 'Lucifer' but has more yellow with a red 'cross' in the centre. Raised in 1892 by G. Ernst.

'Kreta' See Island Series.

'La Bohème' See Grand Opera Series.

'Lafayette' (T) This canna has reflexed, deep scarlet flowers and purple foliage. It is similar to 'Assaut', 'Hercule' and 'Vainquer' and it is difficult to know if these are distinct, although this name was registered by H. Cayeux in 1925.

'La Gloire' (M) This lovely old cultivar has large, pale apricot-salmon flowers with 'toothy' petals. The foliage is bronze. It was raised by Vilmorin-Andrieux in 1920 and is available from a few specialist nurseries.

is not registered and the plant seems to be identical to 'Wyoming'. The nursery that lists it does not offer the latter, suggesting that it has been renamed.

'Liberty' (M) Rose-red flowers and green foliage. It was raised by Longwood Gardens and first flowered in 1976, although it is not widely available as yet. Not to be confused with the Liberty Series below.

Liberty Series™ This recent string of cannas was originally developed by Dr Jack Roberson of the American Daylily and Perennial Company in association with Kent Kelly of the Quality Gladiolus Company. Due to production changes, the name is now solely held by Dr Roberson. Because of the change of legal ownership of the copyrighted names, three of these are also included within the Futurity Series. They are not widely available.

'Liberty™ **Bugle Boy'** (S) This has red-yellow bicoloured flowers with green foliage.

'Liberty™ **Cantaloupe'** (M) The pale cantaloupe flowers are flecked with pink. It has green foliage.

'Liberty™ **Coral Rose'** (syn. 'Rose Futurity') (S) One of the original set, this has deep rose-pink flowers and burgundy foliage.

'Liberty™ **Keylime'** (S) This canna has pale creamy-yellow flowers and green foliage

'Liberty™ **Pink'** (syn. 'Pink Futurity') (S) This is one of the originals of the series. Its rich burgundy foliage makes an excellent foil for the soft pink flowers.

'Liberty™ **Pink Splash'** (S) This is light rose with cream splashes and thin margins to the petals. It is very compact with green foliage.

'Liberty™ **Scarlet'** (S) The bright red flowers are set against bronze foliage.

'Liberty™ **Sun'** (syn. 'Yellow Futurity') (S) Another of the originals with clear yellow flowers covered in soft red spots. The leaf colour is green.

'Liberty™ **Watermelon'** (S) Raspberry-pink flowers are set against green foliage.

'Liebesglut' (M) The flowers of this cultivar are deep crimson. It is very similar to 'Black Knight', and although this name is registered, it is difficult to know whether there is any distinction, or whether this is the correct name. It has dark bluish-bronze foliage and is available from specialist nurseries.

'Lilian Cole' (M) This cultivar produces large, soft apricot flowers with golden centres and ragged petals giving an attractive 'ragamuffin' effect. It has green leaves.

'Lippo's Kiwi' (M) A striking cultivar with bright scarlet flowers and a narrow but slightly jagged yellow margin. The flower has four petals and is slightly rippled. The leaves are green. Not widely available.

'Losotho Lil' (T) This cultivar appeared recently in Britain. It has huge, orange flowers, very similar in appearance to 'Singapore Girl'. The name is not substantiated but has a nice ring to it. Available from a few British nurseries.

'Louis Cayeux' (M) This well-known name belongs to a large, orchid-flowered canna with bright salmon-pink blooms. It is a neat plant with green foliage and looks superb planted with *Phormium* 'Sundowner'. Raised by H. Cayeux in 1924, it is readily available in this form, although it should be said that the 'International Checklist' describes it as 'jasper red'.

'Louis Cottin' (S) Rounded, substantial, trumpet-shaped flowers in burnt copper. Keith Hayward describes them as 'carved in alabaster'. It has sultry dark foliage. This cultivar seems to remain dwarf under almost any conditions.

'Lucifer' (S) One of the best with very short, masses of iris-like, red-yellow bicolour flowers. It is sometimes sold as 'Dwarf Lucifer' to distinguish it from 'Rosemond Coles', which is sometimes wrongly offered under the name 'Lucifer'. Raised by H. Faiss, it is readily available, although stocks do vary with the width of the yellow margin being inconsistent. In cultivation it is sometimes muddled with 'Königin Charlotte', which has more yellow.

'Madame Angele Martin' (T) A lovely old cultivar with flowers in a soft apricot, blushed with rose. The foliage is a pale pewter-bronze. Altogether the effect is very subtle. It was raised by Vilmorin-Andrieux in 1915. Available in British and European nurseries.

'Madame Butterfly' See Grand Opera Series.

'**Madame Paul Casaneuve**' (M) This cultivar has peachy-pink flowers and bronze foliage. It is very similar to 'Madame Angele Martin' and was raised by A. Crozy in 1902.

'**Madeira**' See Island Series.

'**Maggie**' (S) This has large, pink 'twisty' flowers with bronze leaves. It is said to be good for planters. Available from specialist nurseries.

'**Mandarin Orange**' (M) The shapely flowers of this cultivar are very effective, being vivid russet-orange with a pale creamy centre. Each petal is also rimmed with an irregular yellow margin. Petals are attractively rippled and twisted. The foliage is green and the origin is unknown. Very similar to 'Cheerfulness'; neither name is registered.

'**Marie Nagel**' (T) Red, butterfly-shaped flowers with a touch of yellow in the throat are borne in distinct spire-like spikes. It has green foliage.

'**Marjorie Cole**'(M) Another of the Cole cultivars, this one is deep rich salmon-pink with a touch of yellow. The leaves are green. Available from specialist nurseries and in New Zealand.

'**Marvel**' (M) The scarlet, iris-like flowers are not particularly distinct. It has green leaves. The name is registered but there are no details of raiser or date. Not worth searching for.

'**Maudie Malcolm**' (M) Rich cerise-pink flowers are quite rounded with very delicately frilled edges to the petals. The flower centre is ivory and the reverse of the petals is almost white. It is reasonably compact and has a self-cleaning habit. Available in the USA, having been developed as a seedling from 'Rosenkavalier' (see Grand Opera Series) by Patrick Malcolm.

'**Melanie**' See 'Centenaire de Rozain-Boucharlat'.

'**Merle Cole**' (S) This cultivar has huge, red flowers and green leaves with red ribs. Like so many of the Cole cultivars, it is only available from a few specialist nurseries.

The subtle shades of 'Madame Paul Casaneuve' prove that not all cannas are brash.

'**Meyerbeer**' (M) The large, bright canary-yellow flowers of this cultivar are heavily spotted with scarlet lozenge-shaped blotches and borne over bright green leaves. It is probably the brashest of the spotted cannas and generally admired. Fairly easy to obtain.

'**Minerva**' See 'Bankok'.

'**Montaigne**' (M) This sturdy cultivar has gleaming rose-pink flowers over dusky-bronze foliage. Available from Ernest Turc.

'**Mowhawk**' (T) A tall, strong-growing canna with wide, bronze leaves and large, soft orange flowers. This cultivar, available in the USA, seems to be very similar to 'Wyoming'. However, the name is established and it was listed in Vaughan's catalogue of 1928. Without close comparison, it is impossible to say if it is distinct.

'Mrs Oklahoma' (syn. 'Miss Oklahoma', 'Los Angeles', 'Pink President') (T) A lovely cultivar with huge gladiolus-like, rich shrimp-pink flowers with satin-like petals. The plant is sturdy and vigorous with large, green leaves. The incorrect name 'Pink President' shows the desire of some unscrupulous members of the nursery trade to cash in on another well-known name by adding to it! Readily available.

'Mrs Pierre du Pont' (M) This is an old cultivar which is likely to have been named after the owner of Longwood Gardens, Pennsylvania, where it is still grown. The date of introduction is not known, but it was commercially available by 1933, when it was offered by George Mellen and Co in the USA. It has beautifully shaped, clear pink blooms over fresh green foliage and is free flowering with a compact habit. It is not currently available in Britain and rarely seen in commercial outlets in the USA but well worth searching out.

'Mrs Tim Taylor' (T) Huge, fluorescent salmon-orange flowers are well presented on top of a very vigorous, upright plant. A very rich and opulent colour. It has slightly glaucous, paddle-like, green leaves. Available from specialist nurseries.

'Mystique' (T) Mainly grown for its narrow foliage with an iridescent mix of purple, blue and pewter. It has small, cherry-red flowers that contrast well with the leaf colour. Very valuable as a foliage or background plant. It originated in Kew Gardens and I named it as it is worth distributing. Mainly available from specialist nurseries in Britain.

'Nattie Cole' (M) This has deep salmon-apricot flowers with large, rippled petals. It has green foliage and is only available from specialist nurseries.

'Nectarine' (M) Although the name is doubtful, this is well worth acquiring with soft pinkish-salmon flowers in huge, floppy, globose heads above green leaves. It is available from some nurseries in Britain.

'Niagara' (T) A very tall cultivar that has deep cerise flowers and green foliage. Seen in a collection during my visit to the USA. Not readily available.

North Star Series™ These cannas were bred by Reverend Curtis Wallace of North Star, Delaware through his system of line breeding (p.127). The name is trademarked. All are short or medium in height and have green foliage. Sadly, they can be difficult to overwinter and so are easily lost. Very few are readily available from commercial sources.

'**North Star**™ **Arctic**' (S) Large, creamy-white flowers.

'**North Star**™ **Desert Yellow**' (M) Yellow flowers.

'**North Star**™ **Ermine**' (S) White flowers.

'**North Star**™ **Landscape Red**' (S) Clear dark red flowers, very long flowering season. Flowers are held clear of foliage.

'**North Star**™ **Princess**' (M) Coral-pink.

'**North Star**™ **Sweetheart**' (S) Deep red.

'**Nuscantara**' (M) The flowers are a delicate cerise-pink with a little yellow mottling on lip. The individual petals are long, narrow, slightly curved inwards and gently rippled, producing a very elegant flower form. The foliage is green. This is a new cultivar from Malaysia that looks well worth growing further.

'**Oiseau de Feu**' (M) Scarlet flowers are produced over strong green foliage. It is very like 'Fireside', which quite possibly originated from it. It dates from 1911 and was raised by Vilmorin-Andrieux.

'**Oiseau d'Or**' (syn. 'Goldvogel') (M) This has primrose-yellow flowers with pale pink spots. By the second day, it is pale enough to be considered with the almost-whites. It was raised by Vilmorin-Andrieux in 1918.

'**Omega**' (T) Huge, glaucous-green, paddle-like leaves make this a worthwhile inclusion in an exotic planting. The small flowers in soft orange are insignificant. Said to be an improved form of C. 'Heliconifolia', it is very tall growing and has been known to reach nearly 3.9m (13ft) but this is under very warm conditions. Fairly easily available.

'**Orange Beauty**' (T) This classic canna has very large, orange flowers, with some faint yellow streaking in the fluted petals. If a big bright orange canna is required

'North Star Princess' is one of a series of compact cannas raised by Curtis Wallace.

The small butterfly-like flowers of 'Panache' qualify it as one of the most delicate of cannas.

then this is predictable! It is very vigorous, often reaching to more than 2.1m (7ft), with huge, green leaves. It is readily available.

'Orange Perfection' (T) A tall leafy canna that is useful as a background plant and produces smallish orange flowers. Flowering starts early. It grows very tall and has been known to top 3m (10ft) high in generous soil conditions with warmth and water. It is tough and is likely to be one of the hardier types for overwintering outside.

'Orange Punch' (M) The colour of this cultivar is reminiscent of a well-known canned, fizzy orange drink! The rich orange blends into yellow in the throat. It has a long season of flower and is entirely self-cleaning. In hot, dry conditions, the stems are inclined to droop with the weight of flowers, a trait avoided by keeping the plant well watered. The foliage is green.

'Orchid' See 'City of Portland'.

'Pacific Beauty' See 'Sémaphore'.

'Paddy's Red' (T) This is one of a series of similar red cannas with very rich foliage. It bears similarity to 'General Eisenhower', 'Red' and 'Red Cleopatra'. None of these names is registered, but all plants are slightly different, possibly all being mutations of 'Cleopatra'. Despite the ambiguity, all are striking plants. Only available from specialist nurseries and collections.

'Pallag Szépe' (S) The lovely frilly flowers are a sugary blancmange-pink edged with creamy-yellow. This is similar to 'Journey's End' but more pink. It is very compact and stocky with green foliage. It was raised in Hungary in 1966 but is not readily available.

'**Panache**' (T) This lovely canna is quite distinct from almost any other described in this list and proves that not all cannas are brash. It has narrow, glaucous-green leaves and small, very delicate flowers in open trusses. The four petals are long and thin and their wide spacing creates a very open, spidery effect. The colour is a soft apricot, shading to deep pink in the throat. The overriding effect is light and open like a small cloud of delicate moths. It was introduced by Herb Kelly. In France, where *panaché* means variegated, the name is also confusingly used to refer to 'Pretoria' and other variegated cannas.

'**Panama**'® (M) Luminous, large, yellow flowers are produced above a compact plant with green foliage. This cultivar is another new introduction from Ernest Turc.

'**Passionata**' (T) Another plant grown primarily for its foliage having vigorous but narrow leaves of soft pewter-bronze. The blooms are delicate apricot. It is a good background plant and useful with the other small-flowered cannas. Introduced by myself and probably only available in Britain.

'**Peach Blush**' (M) This exquisite cultivar has flowers with a soft candy-stripe effect. The overall colour is rich peach but there are paler pink and also almost-white stripes in each flower. The many flower heads give a good overall display but the individual flowers are well worth close examination. The leaves are green. Another recent introduction from Kent Kelly, but not as yet readily available.

'**Pele**' (S) A newish canna bearing dark orange-red flowers with some yellow markings in the throat. The greyish-green leaves have dark margins. It was raised by Bob Armstrong of Longwood Gardens and first flowered in 1990. Not readily available as yet.

'**Penn**' (M) A canna with reddish-orange flowers and green leaves with burgundy margins. Another one from Longwood Gardens raised in 1985 but not yet readily available.

'**Perkeo**' (M) A very familiar canna with bright pink, iris-like flowers. It is quite compact and reliable. This

'Perkeo' is one of several names for this familiar pink-flowered cultivar.

cultivar is sold under many other names such as 'Evening Star', 'Fatamorgana' and 'Francis Berti'. Both the latter names are registered, but it is currently impossible to verify whether different cultivars actually exist. The original 'Perkeo' was raised by Wilhelm Pfitzer.

'**Petit Poucet**' (S) This canna has vivid canary-yellow, trumpet-shaped flowers with small, red spots, produced in tight heads. It has green leaves and is a very compact plant. Although splendid when it performs well, the flowers do not always open properly and are often lost in the foliage, making this a disappointing cultivar.

'**Pfitzer's Cherry Red**' (M) This cultivar has smallish iris-like, mid-red flowers. It is quite similar to 'Strasbourg' but slightly more towards the orange shadings

Pfitzer's Cherry Red' (above) and Pfitzer's Chinese Coral' (below) are two of the many cultivars raised in Germany by Wilhelm Pfitzer.

and with a touch of yellow on the lip. It has green foliage and a white farina on the stems. Readily available but often sold as 'Cherry Red'.

'Pfitzer's Chinese Coral' (M) There is some confusion about this cultivar. Most stocks are rich coral-pink with slightly creased-looking petals. There is also a more red form available. The foliage of both is green. As with so many of these old cultivars, it is difficult, without more detailed study, to say adamantly which is correct.

'Pfitzer's Primrose Yellow' (S) Many confusing variations on a dwarf yellow are offered under this name. The cultivar is said to be compact and to have pink dots on the primrose petals. It has been impossible at this stage for me to verify the precise description of this one.

'Pfitzer's Salmon Pink' (S) The substantial flowers of this cultivar are an agreeable soft salmon-pink with yellow markings in centre. It has very full ruffled petals. A compact though rather 'heavyweight' plant, it is still well worth growing. It has large, green leaves. Readily available, often just as 'Salmon Pink'.

'Phasion' See 'Durban'.

'Picadore' (M) Tomato-red flowers have a bold yellow throat. The very strong pigmentation in the flower makes this colour quite distinct. It is a compact grower with green leaves. Raised by Ernest Turc, it is generally available only from specialist nurseries.

'Picasso' (M) All stocks of this have soft yellow flowers with light red spots. Although probably the commonest spotted canna, the quality does vary and there are many inferior types, so it is difficult to know what the true 'Picasso' looks like. Readily available but generally not the best of spotted cannas.

'Pink Futurity' See Futurity Series.

'Pink Princess' (M) Another cultivar from Kent Kelly, this one with rich pink blossoms. It is early- and continuous-flowering. The foliage is lance-shaped and green. It is not readily available.

'**Pink Sunburst**' (syn. 'Pringle Bay') (S) This lively, recent introduction has a multicoloured leaf, similar to the 'Durbans' with a rich mix consisting of a deep bottle-green background, overlaid with yellow and pink stripes. Flowers are mid-pink and produced early. The compact habit of growth is retained under most conditions and many would regard this as one of the shortest cannas available today. It is best considered as a foliage plant as the flowers are not freely produced and do not show well above the foliage. Although quite new, it is readily available.

'**Pink Sunrise**' (M) The name for this lovely cultivar is not entirely appropriate. Although there are blushes of light rose and yellow the overriding colour is rich apricot. The throat is a darker, duskier colour and the foliage is green. Another winner from Kent Kelly.

'**Plantagenet**' (M) Flowers are deep strawberry-pink with long, relaxed petals giving an attractive open shape. It has bronze foliage with darker bands.

'**President**' (M) This well-known classic has huge, scarlet, gladiolus-like flowers with a faint yellow edge and some yellow markings in the centre. The leaves are wide and glaucous-green. It is susceptible to roller caterpillars, where these occur. Although reliable, there are undoubtedly better modern cultivars. It is similar to 'Fireside' and a number of others. It was raised in the USA, possibly by Wintzer, in 1923.

'**President Carnot**' (M) The deep-red flowers of this one have some yellow in the throat. It has dark foliage. This old cultivar was originally raised by Crozy sometime before 1889.

'**Pretoria**' (syn. 'Striatum', *malawiensis variegata*, 'Bengal Tiger', 'Panaché' [France]) (M) This is undoubtedly the most popular and well-known of the coloured-leaved cannas and very much a 'love it or hate it' plant. No one can miss the huge, pale green leaves with conspicuous yellow veins and thin purple ribbon edges. The stems have a plum colouring and all is crowned with large, strident orange flowers.

This canna's background is very uncertain. It is said to have originated in India over 50 years ago, hence 'Bengal Tiger'. Apparently Indian merchants brought

The vivid leaves of 'Pretoria' make it the most widely grown foliage canna.

it to Africa, and so the name 'Pretoria'. Various nurseries claim the responsibility for its introduction to the USA. As yet, none of this can be verified. It is the most readily available variegated canna, although because of its popularity, invariably in short supply.

'**Pride of India**' (syn. 'Taj Mahal') (M) Large, rich rose-pink flowers with green foliage.

'**Prince Charmant**' (M) This handsome old cultivar has large, deep watermelon-rose flowers, generously produced. There is a touch of yellow in the throat. The intensity of pigment in this flower makes the colour quite distinct. It has green leaves and a white farina on the flower stem. Raised in 1892 but is only available from specialist nurseries.

'**Princess Di**' (M) The huge inflorescences of soft peachy-cream flowers have a touch of yellow in the

PLATE VI

PINK-FLOWERED CANNAS

'Centenaire de
Rozain-Boucharlat'

'Mrs Oklahoma'

'Rosenkavalier'

'Perkeo'

'City of Portland'

'La Gloire'

'Prince Charmant'

All flowers are shown at approximately half lifesize

'Ruby Cole'

'Saladin'

'Tirol'

'Alberich'

'King Hakon'

'Horn'

centre. This splendid cultivar blooms right through from an early start to the end of the season. The flowers sit well above the lance-shaped, green foliage making a very elegant display. Raised by Kent Kelly but not widely available as yet.

'Professor Lorentz' See 'Wyoming'. This name has been very widely used in Britain but, although registered, it is impossible to know whether it has any validity. 'Wyoming' seems to be more widely accepted.

'Puck' (S) The medium-sized, frilled flowers are pale primrose-yellow with faint purple spots. It is a genuine dwarf plant, although the grey-green foliage is a little heavy and the flowers tend to nestle too tightly into the leaves. It is useful for front of the border or for planters. Fairly available but not particularly desirable.

'Ra' (T) The third of the water cannas, this one having bright lemon-yellow flowers and narrow glaucous foliage. Although similar to its parent C. *glauca*, it is darker and slightly larger-flowered. It is very tall and slender and may reach well over 2.4m (8ft).

'Red Dazzler' (T) A gigantic plant with huge, deep orange, gladiolus-like flowers that are borne atop massive lettuce-green leaves. Similar to 'Wintzer's Colossal', although the name is registered independently. It is very readily available and highly reliable.

'Red King Humbert' (T) This widely grown canna is dark orange rather than pure red. It has deep bronze, paddle-shaped leaves. Despite some confusion in naming (see p.157), it is a very good cultivar and quite possibly the original 'Roi Humbert' of 1902 origins. Quite readily available.

'Red Stripe' (possibly syn. C. 'Indica Purpurea') (T) This is a can't-miss addition to the border. It has 2.4m (8ft) tall stems which are home to large (nearly 60cm/2ft long) leaves of purple with a dramatically contrasting green pattern between the veins. Topping the bold foliage are stalks of small, brilliant red flowers. 'Red Stripe' is very similar to C. 'Indica Purpurea' and as it seeds readily, it is quite likely to be a variation on it. Available from specialist nurseries, especially in the USA.

Despite the confusion on naming, 'Roi Humbert' is a splendid cultivar with rich bronze foliage.

'Red Wine' (M) The rich burgundy-coloured foliage of this cultivar is one of its main features. This is topped by large, wine-red flowers, which are copiously produced. It has a good self-cleaning habit. Raised by Kent Kelly.

'Reine Charlotte' See 'Königin Charlotte'.

'Richard Wallace' (syn. 'King Midas') (M) Flowers are a strong clear yellow with a few light red spots in the throat and lightly frilled petals. The leaves are bright apple-green and it has a vigorous but not tall habit. Its garden performance is reliable and it is easy to grow. It was raised in 1902 by Wilhelm Pfitzer and is readily available.

The name 'King Midas' is actually separately registered but both names seem to be universally used for the same clone. There is also a form available in France with nicely shaped, clear pale primrose-yellow flowers that have slight purple spotting. The name is unlikely to be correct, although the latter is a good plant.

'Rigoletto' See Grand Opera Series.

'Robert Kemp' (T) Lush green foliage makes this a good background plant. The flowers are small and dark orange. It is a prolific grower and sadly often substituted for more desirable types by unscrupulous nurserymen. It is, therefore, readily available but often not under its true name. Don't search for it – sooner or later it will find you! In parts of the USA, it is sometimes called the 'outhouse canna' because of its value in the past for screening a certain small building.

'Roi Humbert' (T) Tomato-red flowers suffused orange and gold. This exceedingly tall cultivar has deep glossy brown foliage. A further confusion of this old name: this is not the same as 'King Humbert' or 'Red King Humbert'. This particular form is available from Pierre Turc in France.

'Roi Soleil' (M) This aristocratic plant has vivid cardinal-red flowers with gold markings in the throat. Each flower is quite large with a frilly edge to the petals. The stems are soft purple and bear deep glossy green leaves. It was raised in 1930 by Vilmorin-Andrieux. Relatively easy to obtain.

'Roitelot' (S) A cultivar with bright capsicum-red flowers, which are tinted orange. It is early flowering and has green foliage. It is one of the best dwarf types and was raised by G. Truffaut in 1966. It is generally available from specialist nurseries.

'Rosalinda' (M) This cultivar has yellow flowers that are streaked with red rays from the throat. It is quite sensational and very beautiful. Green foliage. It is available in the USA.

'Rose Futurity' See Futurity Series.

'Rosemond Coles' (M) Another of those classic cannas that has been grown in vast numbers in the past. It has large, bold, green leaves and the flowers are large and clear red with wide yellow petal margins and spots in the throat. There is no question that it is very big and bright. It is a strong grower and fairly reliable. However, the flower heads are not always tidy, dead flowers tending to bunch up and go mushy. It is often wrongly offered in the trade as 'Lucifer'. Very widely available but by modern standards is a poor cultivar.

The luscious pink flowers of 'Ruby Cole' are laced and backed with cream colourings.

'Rosenkavalier' See Grand Opera Series.

'Ruby Cole' (M) This exquisite cultivar is generally only available in New Zealand and from a few private collectors. It has large, full, gladiolus-like flowers in deep smoky pink with distinct, slightly ragged, lemon-yellow edges. There are yellow markings in the centre of the flower and on the back of the petals. The leaves are green. It is very distinct and highly desirable.

'Saladin' (M) This is one of the best of the deep pinks with dark foliage. The sugar-pink flowers have darker spotting in the throat and a fine red margin to each of the petals. Narrow petals that do not overlap give the flower a light, airy effect. It has bronze foliage. Becoming more widely available in Britain and Europe.

'Salmon Pink' See 'Pfitzer's Salmon Pink'.

'Saumur' (M) A French cultivar with tangerine-coloured, iris-like flowers and bronze foliage. It is like 'Verdi'. Not widely available and not distinct enough to be desirable.

'**Schwäbische Heimat**' (M) Bright carmine flowers are borne above green foliage. This old cultivar was raised by Wilhelm Pfitzer in 1895 and is still available from Podgora Gardens in New Zealand.

'**Sémaphore**' (syn. 'Pacific Beauty') (M) Any good canna collection should include this cultivar as it is the nearest to a yellow with dark foliage. The chrome yellow-orange, iris-like flowers are borne in narrow heads with pinkish stems. The foliage is a strange bluish-bronze. The habit of growth is quite slender. This lovely old cultivar was raised by Vilmorin-Andrieux in 1895 and it seems amazing that in the 106 years since then there have been no other yellows with dark foliage. It is reasonably easy to obtain and well worth growing.

'**Shenandoah**' (M) Another wonderful historic cultivar. The magnificent, shapely flowers graduate from deep pink to almost ruby at the centre. Rich ruby foliage with a white farina contrasts beautifully with

the brilliant flowers. It was raised by A. Wintzer in 1894 and is still one of the best available. It is generally only available from specialist nurseries and is always in short supply.

'**Shining Pink**' See 'Pink Futurity'.

'**Singapore Girl**' (T) This is a colossal plant with gigantic, green leaves. Massive gladiolus-like flowers are produced in two-tone 'ice-lolly' orange. Very upright, it is a vigorous grower, in a good summer reaching to over 2.1m (7ft). It is reasonably easy to obtain.

'**Soudan**' (T) This cultivar has large, soft orange flowers and purple foliage. It is very like 'Wyoming' and quite possibly identical. The name is separately registered. It is generally available in France.

'**Stadt Fellbach**' (M) This has large heads of flowers in rich apricot-pink with creamy-yellow markings in the centre. The heads are quite loose giving a shaggy effect. It is quite vigorous and bushy with plain green leaves. It was raised by Wilhelm Pfitzer in 1934 and is reasonably easy to obtain.

'**Statue of Liberty**' (T) A mammoth plant with hefty, soft red flowers. The stem is crowded with huge, purple leaves and it is very tall. It is quite comparable to 'Wintzer's Colossal'. It is only available from very few sources, including New Zealand. The date of introduction is unknown, although it is described in Vaughan's catalogue of 1928.

'**Strasbourg**' (M) Although familiar, this is a chirpy little canna with freely produced, bright cherry-red, iris-like flowers. It is reliable and compact with small, narrow, green leaves delicately ribboned in maroon. Very much a plant to be used in the front of the border. Raised by Wilhelm Pfitzer and widely available.

'**Striatum**' See 'Pretoria'.

'**Striped Beauty**' See 'Bankok'.

Surviving from 1895, 'Sémaphore' is distinct as the only yellow cultivar with dark foliage.

The volume of flower produced by 'Singapore Girl' makes it a cultivar worthy of mass planting.

'Stuttgart' (syn. C. 'Striata') (T) This potentially beautiful cultivar is derived from C. 'Heliconifolia'. The foliage is long and slender in pale sea-green with irregular silver and white markings. However, it is rarely seen without scorch marks. To avoid bad scorching, it really needs to be grown in light shade and with adequate moisture, and even then it sometimes succumbs. Growing to about 2m (6½ft), it is eventually topped by small, apricot flowers. Its variability means that it is prone to reversion to the plain green form. Adequate stock should always be grown to allow for selection of good forms. It was imported to the USA by the late Bob Hayes of Brooklyn Botanic Gardens, from the Stuttgart Botanic Garden. Generally widely available.

'Südfunk' (S) Large, gaudy orange-red flowers over bronze foliage. This canna is early and free flowering. Its compact habit makes it good for planters. Raised by Wilhelm Pfitzer in 1930. Not readily available.

'Sunny Delight' (M) Bright yellow blooms are produced over lush green foliage on sturdy plants. Blooming starts early and is continuous and prolific. It has some self-cleaning ability. Available in the USA.

'Tabitha Cole' (M) Another from the prodigious Australian breeder Cole. This has large, frilly, soft yellow flowers with soft red blotches. Leaves are green. Really only available from specialist nurseries.

'Tafraout' (S) Cherry-red flowers are freely produced on a compact plant with green foliage. Available from Ernest Turc.

'Tropical Sunrise' has a lovely mix of soft colours that never seem to be the same in any two flowers.

'Talisman' (M) This distinctive cultivar has pale lemon-yellow flowers with pencilled red markings. It is similar to 'Heinrich Seidel' but earlier flowering. Each of the green leaves has a dark margin and twisted tip. The name is registered but it is not readily available.

'Taney' (T) The fourth of the quartet of water cannas. This one has clear apricot-orange, iris-like flowers. It is tall and lax with narrow, glaucous-green leaves. Like the others, it was raised by Longwood Gardens. It is reasonably easy to obtain but perhaps less widely distributed than the other three water cannas.

'Tango' (T) Flowers are red-orange with a distinct yellow frill and a spotted throat. It has pointed green leaves and is reasonably vigorous. Although named by me, it was raised by Peter Edgar. Limited availability in Britain.

'Taroudant' (M) This compact plant bears medium-sized, iris-like, golden-yellow flowers, suffused and blotched with red-orange. A fine bicoloured cultivar with green leaves. Raised by Ernest Turc, it is available from specialist nurseries.

'Tchad' (M) The dark red flowers of this cultivar are borne over purple foliage. It is very similar to 'Assaut'. Available in France.

'Tirol' (T) There are two similar but distinct clones available under this name. Both have large, deep salmon-pink flowers and green leaves with purple tinges. One has a slightly darker rim to the edge of the flower and darker almost bronze foliage. The original one was raised by Wilhelm Pfitzer in 1930. It is impossible at this stage to say which is correct. Stocks of both types are generally available.

'Triumph' (syn. 'Triomphe') (M) This has large, tangerine-orange flowers produced over bronze foliage. It could be the 1920 cultivar introduced by Vilmorin-Andrieux. Not readily available.

'Tropical Rose' (S) A chunky little plant with medium-sized, sugar-pink flowers and green foliage. It is of interest in that it is one of a new generation of true-breeding seed-raised cannas. It was raised by Takii & Co of Japan and developed by the subsidiary American Takii of Salinas and first released in 1991 to be subsequently awarded the All America Selections (AAS) award. It takes approximately 90 days to flower from seed sowing. There is also 'Tropical Red', which is less commonly available and does not perform so well. Usually obtainable from garden centres each summer.

'Tropical Sunrise' (M) Large flowers are elegant pale pink but can appear darker or near white, depending on the light. Substantial flowers in rounded heads.

'Tropicanna'™ See 'Durban'.

'Vainquer' (T) Another cultivar with deep scarlet flowers and purple foliage. It resembles 'Assaut', 'Lafayette' and 'Hercule' but, in this case, the name is not registered. Generally only available from specialist nurseries and in France.

'Valentine' (M) The flowers of this striking cultivar are an intense blood-red, while the flowering stems are purplish with a white farina, giving an overall stunning effect. The plant is compact with dark green leaves. It is generally self-cleaning. Yet another Kent Kelly introduction but as yet not widely available.

'Vera Cole' (M) The large, orange-apricot flowers are borne over green foliage. Can only be obtained from specialist nurseries.

'Verdi' (M) A first-class classic cultivar. It has iris-shaped, vivid tangerine flowers with yellow markings in the throat. Together with the bronze-veined leaves, it is a striking combination of foliage and flower. Quite compact. Raised by L. Kapiteyn and widely available.

'Vermilion' (M) The vivid orange-red flowers are reminiscent of the 'Verdi', and it also has bronze foliage. One more from the stable of Kent Kelly. Not as yet widely available.

'Viva'® (M) Large, bright red, smooth-petalled flowers are freely produced by this recent introduction from Ernest Turc. It has huge, slender, purple leaves. Not readily available.

'Wine 'n Roses' (M) This cultivar bears a similarity to 'Red Wine'. Blossoms are large and coloured a deep rose-red over dark burgundy foliage. From specialist nurseries, and at present generally only in the USA.

'Wintzer's Colossal' (T) A classic cultivar, not surprisingly raised by Wintzer. It makes an enormous plant with gigantic, deep crimson flowers and massive paddle-like green leaves. Well worth growing to make a strong statement! Available from specialist nurseries.

'Wyoming' (T) Probably the best known of all bronze-leaved cannas. It bears huge, soft orange flowers on top of vigorous plants with massive dark-veined leaves. This cultivar was raised by Wintzer in 1906.

Confusingly, the name is sometimes used for any orange canna with dark leaves. In Britain, there are at least three different forms available under this name. Probably the most correct is the one that has for many years also be sold under the name 'Professor Lorentz'. It

'Vera Cole' is one of a number of cultivars raised by the Australian breeder Cole and is slowly becoming available.

is very vigorous and makes a tall bold plant sometimes nearing 2.4m (8ft). It is widely available.

'Yellow Humbert' (M) A confusing name that is often used and attached to various cultivars such as 'Cleopatra', 'Florence Vaughan' and 'Richard Wallace'. The name is registered and the 'International Checklist' describes a cultivar with red stripes, which does not fit any of the above. Best avoided!

'Zebra Cole' (M) A nicely shaped, spotty yellow. The spoon-like petals are a clear yellow with red spots. It has green foliage. It is quite nice but nothing distinct and not readily available.

Zulu Series These were raised by Mrs Sheppard who used to have a nursery in Texas. They are now distributed by Kelly's Plant World (Herb Kelly) but not widely grown. Mrs Sheppard raised various cannas but prefixed all her bronze-leaved introductions with 'Zulu'. All are said to be strong growing.

'Zulu Apricot Nectar' (M) Light apricot flowers.
'Zulu Maiden' (T) Red with darker red spots.
'Zulu Masquerade' (T) Orange red with yellow streaks.
'Zulu Princess' (T) Mid-pink.
'Zulu Queen' (T) Pink.
'Zulu Warrior' (T) Orange.

7

CANNAS IN THE GARDEN

As components in any landscape or planting scheme, cannas make a very conspicuous and generally bold contribution. The leaves are huge with a paddle-like shape producing a very strong textural effect and their glossiness in many cultivars means that they reflect light easily. The stout, upright habit and stature of many canna cultivars also contributes to their dominant nature. In landscape terms, cannas are regarded as plants with a solid structure: they are often best used as powerful accent plants in big bold clumps, contrasted against other planting with smaller or narrow leaves or of low stature. Cannas are plants that demand to be noticed!

FLOWERS

In considering colour, cannas have a reputation for being strident and, indeed, many cultivars do have huge flowers in very bright, strident shades. They shout! For example, the bright scarlet of 'President' is not for the faint-hearted but is a clear no-nonsense colour. The flower colours emphasize the extrovert nature of the plants. Theirs is a bold palette of such intense colour that it must be used with daring to be effective: small groups of cannas or individual plants may only produce small, spotty blobs of intrusive colour; to be effective, they must be in reasonably sized groups.

All this having been said, there are many, perhaps lesser-known cultivars and species that have both smaller and more delicately coloured flowers. Cannas such as 'Panache', with its delicate apricot-yellow

Canna 'Assaut' flanked by *Dahlia* 'Moonfire', red begonias and *Helichrysum petiolare*.

nodding flowers, would satisfy any pastel enthusiast. The water cannas, together with *C. glauca*, are also dainty and their overall habit is more willowy and graceful. They can also be grown successfully in a moist border. Most of the species cannas have diminutive flowers and *C. iridiflora* 'Ehemanii' has blooms which, although quite large, are somewhat more graceful and pendent than usual, giving a more subtle effect. These delicate cannas might be considered easier to integrate with other plants than the brasher types.

FOLIAGE

For their leaves alone, cannas are worthwhile constituents in a planting scheme. Foliage colour is quite wide. As well as green or bronze leaves, there are numerous variegated types. The dark-leaved cultivars undoubtedly have the strongest presence in a planting scheme. The colouring varies between the rich brown of 'Australia', through various shades of purple to a soft manila overlaid with a pewter-like hue in 'Madame Angele Martin' and others.

Dark foliage should be used with care: too many dark-leaved plants can be oppressive, just as can an excess of dark flowers. Balance a dark-leaved scheme with lighter flowers and silver foliage. One of my favourite combinations is the small-leaved *Helichrysum petiolare*, either the silver-leaved species or the lemon-green cultivar 'Limelight', coupled with any of the dark-leaved cannas. The contrast of both colour and foliage size is very effective.

Site is important with all dark-leaved plants. The dark-leaved cannas are lost in a shady situation and just look dull. Indeed in shady conditions, the dark

Cannas with ricinus, plectranthus and artichokes in an exotic-style display at Michigan State University.

colouring disappears and the leaves become more green. However, with bright sun behind them, shining through the leaves, they fairly glow.

In cannas, green foliage varies between a bright apple-green of 'King Midas', through a duller cabbage-green like 'Italia', to the glaucous, almost grey foliage of the water cannas. Among the green-leaved types, there are several with insignificant flowers – for example, 'Robert Kemp' – that make good background plants. The speed of growth is such that a good lush 1.8m (6ft) background or 'hedge' can be created in a season. However, this is probably an exceptional use for cannas as they generally prefer to be at the front of the stage.

Among the variegated cannas is some of the brightest foliage in the plant world. 'Durban', for example, with its deep purple leaves vividly striped with strawberry-pink, is not a retiring plant: it should be used for what it is, a gaudy eye-catcher! The other variegated types are a little less brash, but all need to be located carefully in a planting scheme as all are

dominant. Occasionally, particularly with the variegated cannas, it may be appropriate to use a foliage type and remove its flowers if they spoil the scheme.

EXOTIC PLANTINGS

Lush groups of plants with spiky foliage, together with those with big bold leaves, all planted with jungle-like abandon are characteristic of an exuberant style, known as exotic. This technique of planting, last popular in the late nineteenth century, has achieved a long-awaited revival in recent years. No doubt there is a significant response to fashion and the media, but the recent warm summers and mild winters have meant that many plants once regarded as tender can be grown outside with great success and to reasonable maturity. Particular exponents are Will Giles, whose recent book *The New Exotic Garden* gives many ideas for creating gardens in this style, and Miles Challis, who has written a number of books on the subject.

Cannas are an essential ingredient of such plantings for their fast growth, ample leaves and bright colours. Some of the easier, commoner cannas can be used as fast-growing background plants and will rapidly achieve well over 1.8m (6ft). 'Robert Kemp', 'Intrigue', C. 'Indica Purpurea' and C. 'Edulis' will romp away, producing copious vegetation in no time at all. One of the most appropriate cannas for an exotic border must be C. 'Musifolia'. As its name suggests, the leaves are like those of a banana, big and lush, and the plant will easily achieve 2.1m (7ft) or more in a season. It rarely flowers under temperate conditions and should be considered for its foliage only. Perhaps even better is the hybrid C. 'Grande', which seems to be easier to grow and overwinter and has slightly wavy leaves with pronounced purple margins and midribs.

This style also makes use of hardy exotics, including the hardy palm *Trachycarpus fortunei*, *Phormiun tenax*, better known as New Zealand flax, in all its many forms, spiky yuccas, bamboos and all the coloured types of *Cordyline australis*. These permanent structure plants provide the perfect foil for the seasonal addition of cannas and various other tender plants, including bronze-leaved *Ricinus* 'Carmencita', abutilons, agaves and the tree-like *Dahlia imperialis*.

Large bold blocks planted in deep borders is the best way of creating an exotic atmosphere, although there are some very effective tropical gardens in small spaces – tiny leafy oases.

Generally, as with their use generally in gardens, the cannas need to be placed where they will give a contrast to surrounding foliage and flowers. C. 'Musifolia' is most effective planted in big background groups, whereas 'Durban', with its eye-catching foliage colours, is best planted nearer the front of the border as a statement.

A successful combination that has been seen in several gardens in recent years is 'Pretoria', with its stripy yellow foliage, alongside the deep, almost black foliage and scarlet flowers of *Lobelia* 'Queen Victoria'. Of similar colouring is the lovely old cultivar *Dahlia* 'Bishop of Llandaff' with almost black leaves and single scarlet flowers. It associates perfectly with C. 'Warszewiczii', which has tiny scarlet flowers and green leaves with ruby margins.

Another effective mixture is dark purple-leaved, red-flowered 'Hercule' contrasted with the silvery cut leaves of *Centaurea gymnocarpa* and the livid red-leaved *Iresine herbstii* 'Brilliantissima'. This scheme could be extended with the shorter, red-flowered canna 'President' and surrounded by the silvery filigreed leaves of *Helichrysum petiolare*.

The lovely tall, rich purple, almost iridescent-leaved canna called 'Mystique' is often found in subtropical plantings. It associates well with *Cleome spinosa*, the pink spider flower, the light feathery trails of *Arundo donax* 'Variegata' and the velvety silver leaves of *Plectranthus argentatus*.

A less contrived effect, without an excess of flowers, relies on lush shades of green from plants such as *Trachycarpus fortunei*, bamboos and cordylines, together with cannas such as C. 'Musifolia', C. 'Edulis' and C. 'Heliconifolia', which all provide verdant foliage without intrusive flowers.

Plants to Associate with Cannas in Exotic Plantings

Arundo donax 'Variegata'
Astelia chathamica
Centaurea cineraria subsp. *cineraria* (*Centaurea gymnocarpa*)
Coleus hybrids (*Solenostemon*)
Colocasia esculenta 'Black Magic'
Cordyline australis
Dahlia 'Bishop of Llandaff'
Dahlia imperialis
Dahlia 'Moonfire'
Dicksonia antarctica
Ensete ventricosum (banana)
Fargesia murieliae (bamboo)
Hedychium cultivars (gingers)
Helichrysum petiolare
Helichrysum petiolare 'Limelight'
Iresine herbstii 'Aureoreticulata'
Iresine herbstii 'Brilliantissima'
Lobelia 'Queen Victoria'
Melianthus major
Musa basjoo
Pelargonium (coloured-leaved types)
Plectranthus argentatus
Ricinus communis 'Carmencita'
Sparrmannia africana
Trachycarpus fortunei (hardy palm)
Zantedeschia aethiopica 'Crowborough'

Lobelia 'Queen Victoria' with *Canna* 'Pretoria' in a well tested but still striking mix.

BEDDING

Historically, cannas were first displayed back in the nineteenth century, as dramatic bedding-out plants. Sadly, they are too often seen today as single straggly dot plants in poorly designed municipal bedding. Dot plants are the statements or focal points in a formal bedding display and, as such, cannas should be used in hefty groups. Their height, bold texture and brash flowers make them ideal for floral exclamation marks. In a formal geometric scheme, they can be placed to add height and contrast to lower carpeting plants.

In other countries, the more compact cultivars are used as forthright bedding plants on their own. Cannas such as 'Richard Wallace', 'Lucifer',

'Strasbourg' and 'Louis Cottin' make stunning displays in large beds. Recent breeding programmes have produced a number of new dwarf cultivars eminently suitable for this purpose. Hopefully, such types as the Futurity Series, 'Champigny', 'Maggie' and 'Albricht' will soon be widely sold. To be appreciated as a carpet rather than as a sentinel dot plant, cannas need to be well below eye height, which means that selection must be made from those growing to 90cm (3ft) or less. Many of the new cultivars from the USA will be highly suitable for this when they become available.

A winning scheme, that I saw recently in the USA, used a wide range of brightly coloured primary colours in a rainbow of informality. Orange zinnias, yellow argyranthemums, purple iresine and red impatiens all jostled around the bases of a mix of purple- and

Massed dwarf cannas in a German park, grown as a simple but spectacular bedding display.

green-leaved cannas. All the colours were hot. Such a bold mix was successful as it had a certain theme of exclusion: there was no blue or pink.

A few very effective schemes are described below.

Red and Silver

Canna 'Assaut' with its purple foliage and scarlet flowers would go well with red *Begonia semperflorens* interplanted with silvery *Helichrysum petiolare*. A further layer of flowers could be added with the small red-flowered *Dahlia* 'Bednall Beauty' interplanted in blocks among the begonias.

Pink and White

The rich cerise flowers of *Canna* 'Saladin' associate perfectly with the similarly coloured *Verbena* 'Sissinghurst'. A white daisy-flowered *Argyranthemum* would both lighten and set off the dark foliage of the canna. For a real contrast, add the lime-green *Nicotiana langsdorfii*.

Yellow and Blue

'Richard Wallace' is a good, medium-sized and reliable yellow canna that makes a fine dot plant. It goes well with blue petunias, which in turn could be interplanted with the delicate yellow-flowered *Bidens ferrulaefolia* or the foliage of *Helichrysum petiolare* 'Limelight'.

Orange and White

One of the most vigorous of cannas is 'Wyoming' with rich bronze leaves and opulent orange flowers. This contrasts well with the white foliage of *Abutilon* 'Souvenir de Bonne', which also has orange flowers. A carpet of rich rusty-red French marigolds interplanted with white antirrhinums would complete the scheme.

Crimson and Maroon

One of the most striking displays I have seen recently comprised a bold planting of the deep blood-red *Canna* 'Black Knight'. Behind it were wigwams of a scrambling legume called the hyacinth bean, *Dolichos lablab* 'Ruby Moon'. This has two-tone pink flowers and purplish-black pea-like pods. Around the base was planted a carpet of a lavender verbena. Unexpected colour mixes can be very exciting.

CANNAS IN MIXED AND HERBACEOUS BORDERS

There are very few other plants that are able to provide quite the same theatrical impact in a mixed border planting as cannas. Such borders are traditionally planted principally with permanent shrubs and herbaceous plants, although tender perennials, bulbs and even hardy annuals may be added for variety or to fill a gap in the main framework. Because of their speed of growth, cannas are excellent gap-fillers but, as has been said before, they are also bold plants and in a short space of time become strong focal points. For this reason, they should be used cautiously in borders.

Gertrude Jekyll, one of the most revered designers in the English gardening style of the first half of the twentieth century, used cannas in her plantings. She described them as having the 'handsomest foliage in the border' and placed them so that the light would come through the dark leaves. Jekyll often referred to plants using a description rather than full botanical name so it is possible to recreate her designs using the cultivars available today. In one of her schemes she planted red cannas with bronze foliage, among dark claret-red hollyhocks, rich red dahlias, orange-red phlox, scarlet penstemons and a dwarf red salvia. Among these fiery colourings were patches of deep yellow *Coreopsis lanceolata* and the light, fluffy, white *Gypsophila paniculata*. The group was backed with tall, yellow perennial sunflowers. In another scheme she mixed *Lilium longiflorum*, variegated *Mentha rotundifolia*, golden feverfew, *Calceolaria amplexicaulis*, white, lemon and yellow snapdragons, primrose-yellow African marigolds and yellow cannas. Today's designers might frown at the use of 'common' bedding plants, such as the marigolds, with aristocratic lilies!

The famous red border at Hidcote in Gloucestershire uses cannas. In this garden, which was created by Lawrence Johnson, red poppies, verbena, bronze cordyline and the dark-leaved corylus are planted alongside huge clumps of a deep blood-red canna with bronze leaves. Traditionally, 'King Humbert' is used.

In recent years, great blocks of cannas have been placed in the long borders at the RHS gardens in Wisley, Surrey. Good culture and ample water has resulted in splendid growth of types such as *C.*

PLATE VII

ORANGE-FLOWERED CANNAS

'Cleopatre'

'General Eisenhower'

'Talia' (stem)

'Pallag Szépe'

'Louis Cottin'

'Liberation'

*All flowers are shown at
approximately half lifesize*

'Taroudant'

'Singapore Girl'

'Gaiety'

'Aranályom'

'Madame Angele
Martin'

'Nectarine'

'Wyoming'

iridiflora 'Ehemanii' and 'Pretoria', producing a result that is well in scale with those huge borders. At Rosemore in Devon, also owned by the RHS, blocks of orange-flowered 'Wyoming' form intense focal points in the 'hot garden'.

At Great Dixter, Christopher Lloyd uses cannas in his mixed borders with many other, sometimes unexpected, species. Not surprisingly, dark-leaved cannas mix well with the rich flame colourings of red hot pokers but then in the same picture is shrieking pink *Verbena bonariensis*, the papal mauve of *Eupatorium purpureum* and rugged native teasles. Christopher Lloyd scorns designers that contrive colour schemes and as a result his garden has some astounding plant mixes. Foliage is used liberally, which softens some of the more strident colour combinations. Maybe the sheer variety of plants mingled together means that some striking alliances are bound to occur. Whatever the reason, it works.

PLANNING FOR CANNAS IN BORDERS

In mixed plantings, be sure to use cannas in large enough groups. They should never be placed as individual plants: the effect is thin and lacks impact. In a small private garden with borders of say 2m (7ft) width, groups of three or five are probably adequate; bigger areas will require larger numbers. Sometimes it may be appropriate to site the taller species at the back of a border, where they will fit in with other vigorous species. Planted like this, they become part of the overall picture without dominating. However, if placed nearer to the front, they will make more of a statement.

When planting cannas among existing herbaceous plants and shrubs, choose those cultivars that have enough vigour to compete with the surrounding plants: 'Pretoria', 'Wyoming', 'King Midas', 'En Avant', Miss Oklahoma', 'King Humbert', 'President' and *C. iridiflora* 'Ehemani' would all perform well.

The preparation for planting cannas in a mixed border is just as important as for any other planting, perhaps even more so because of the possible competition. The spot must be well loosened, avoiding damage to neighbouring plants, and plenty of organic matter incorporated. A base fertilizer must be applied before planting, although if the whole border has been treated, this may not be necessary.

The cannas should be of a good size before planting in early summer as the adjacent plants will also be advanced and there will be competition for water, nutrients and light.

SOME COMBINATIONS

This is the ideal situation in which to try both intimate and ambitious combinations with other species such as annual climbers. *Mina lobata*, a small climber with yellow-orange flowers, looks superb scrambling through the dark leaves of an orange-flowered canna such as 'Wyoming'. *Thunbergia alata*, black-eyed Susan, is another scrambler that will clothe cannas without smothering them. The pale lemon-yellow version looks particularly handsome against dark-leaved cannas. Deep purple morning glory, *Ipomoea purpurea*, would look quite arresting growing through the silvery leaves of *Canna glauca*.

Grasses and similar plants associate well with cannas, their narrow ribbon-like foliage fluttering gently against the more upstanding broad leaves of the cannas. Many grasses have pale or variegated foliage so combinations with dark-leaved cannas are likely to be successful. The most spectacular of all is *Arundo donax* 'Variegata', a slightly tender cultivar that produces long waterfall-like leaves, dramatically variegated in white. The plant can grow to over 1.8m (6ft) and each leaf can be up to 45cm (18in) long. Planted with 'Assaut', the effect is stunning from the beginning, but reaches a finale when the deep maroon canna flowers emerge. Other variegated grasses include *Phalaris arundinacea* 'Feesey', a good form of the old gardener's garters. It is easier to grow, and less expensive. There is also *Miscanthus sinensis* 'Variegata', which is more delicate and upright and less likely to be invasive. Try it with 'Shenandoah', a dark-leaved canna with rich cerise blooms. The diminutive yellow sedge *Carex oshimensis* 'Evergold' makes a good companion for the shorter-growing canna 'Richard Wallace'. *Carex secta* var. *tenuiculmis* has wiry, warm brown foliage and would complement any brown-leaved canna – 'Verdi' for example. A touch of contrasting silver from *Helichrysum petiolare* will avoid any heaviness. At Longwood Gardens,

An unexpected combination of an orange canna with *Mina lobata* and *Verbena bonariensis*.

Philadelphia, USA, the pale creamy 'Chesapeake' is planted with feathery grasses and the white-flowered *Aruncus dioicus* 'Kneiffii', giving a very soft luminous effect.

Plant associations should take account of the fact that cannas do not reach their peak or full height until late in the season. Late-flowering perennials such as kniphofia, helenium, hemerocallis, *Eupatorium purpureum*, *Cimcifuga simplex* and dahlias are likely to make the best partners. Remember that most cannas are big, bold creatures and need similar companions. Diminutive herbaceous perennials like dianthus would be lost in direct association with most cannas, although such plants could be used in large numbers to provide a low carpet from which the cannas could emerge as a prominent statement. For example, a carpet of *Lamium* 'Beacon Silver' with its silvery variegated foliage and pink flowers would be an admirable foil for 'Saladin', which has purple foliage and sugar-pink flowers. This is a departure from a traditional mixed border towards a more architectural style of planting, a sort of contemporary bedding using a wide palette of plants.

As most of the other plants in a mixed border will be permanent, it may be appropriate to leave cannas in place at the end of the growing season and hope that they will survive overwinter without lifting. A deep mulch will be needed to help protect the roots from frost (see p.33).

Herbaceous Plants and Grasses to Associate with Cannas

Acanthus spinosus
Achillea 'Moonshine'
Agapanthus Headbourne hybrids
Aruncus dioicus 'Kneiffii'
Cimcifuga simplex
Cortaderia selloana 'Sunningdale Silver' (pampas grass)
Crambe cordifolia
Echinacea purpurea 'Robert Bloom'
Eryngium × *oliverianum*
Eupatorium purpureum
Euphorbia characias
Helictotrichon sempervirens
Hemerocallis 'Kwanso Variegated'
Hemerocallis 'Stafford'

Canna 'Lenape' with herbaceous perennials and grasses in a mixed border at Longwood Gardens.

Hosta 'Thomas Hogg'
Kniphofia 'Percy's Pride'
Kniphofia 'Royal Standard'
Ligularia przewalskii
Macleaya microcarpa 'Kelways Coral Plume'
Miscanthus sinensis 'Variegatus'
Phalaris arundinacea 'Feesey'
Rudbeckia fulgida 'Goldsturm'
Stipa gigantea
Thalictrum delavayi 'Hewitt's Double'

CANNAS IN PLANTERS

A planter is, in effect, a small, raised flowerbed so, theoretically, any style of planting can be used. However, most planters are filled with a combination of bedding plants, which can include cannas. Planters are usually used as key focal points within a garden or landscape, so such plantings usually need to be bold and well coordinated. Once again, cannas will provide height and emphasis. There is, of course, no limit to the size of these containers and there will undoubtedly be those that can take even the biggest of cannas, but for most purposes, the more compact cultivars will be the most suitable. Among the cultivars produced in recent years are many that are not only compact but also early flowering and, therefore, eminently suitable for containers. An attractive combination would be a canna as a sentinel, with shorter plants to bulk out the display and then trailing plants to soften the container's sides.

In a small patio container, for example, 'Südfunk', with orange flowers and dark leaves, could be combined with an orange-flowered gazania such as G. 'Bicton Orange' and trailing *Tropaeolum* 'Hermine Grashoff'. *Helichrysum petiolare* is ideal for providing additional foliage and complementing the silver filigree leaves of the gazania.

For a more stylized planting in a large container try a group of three or five of 'Intrigue', grown mainly for its iridescent purple foliage. Underplant these with several silvery *Plectranthus argentatus*. In bigger pots, there is no reason why two different types of canna cannot be grouped together. For example, the tall foliage of 'Grande' would work very well underplanted with the shorter and floriferous 'Strasbourg', the cherry-red flowers of the latter picking out the ruby ribbons on the edge of the leaves of the former.

JUST CANNAS

Many growers enjoy growing cannas on their own, either because they have a collection of different types or just because they like the voluptuous beauty of a banquet of cannas. Cannas all mixed together do produce a brilliant jewel-like effect with their huge multicoloured heads of flowers. In such displays, the only real need is to ensure that the taller types go towards the rear of the border and the compact ones to the front, where they will not be lost or smothered. In addition, randomly mixing the dark-leaved types in with the green, and adding a smattering of variegated plants, avoids any feeling of repetition.

It is easy to plan a canna border with colour groupings. For example, the tall *C. iridiflora* 'Ehemanii', with its nodding cerise flowers and green foliage, makes a picturebook backdrop for the shorter 'Shenandoah', which has slightly paler pink flowers and deep ruby

foliage. One might also want to separate them into different types for the purpose of study. Grouping together all the historic types, the developments from a certain breeder or maybe all the so-called 'whites' would all make an interesting and informative display.

An old Victorian trick that is worth experimenting with is to create a canna bed interplanted with gladiolus. At first glance, the flowers of gladiolus are very similar to cannas but they are produced earlier and so the result is a display of look-alike flowers among genuine canna foliage, followed by the real thing later in the season. Bristol Zoological Gardens, in southern England, used to produce very effective beds in this way. For a good display it is necessary to start the gladiolus in pots of several bulbs, so that they can be planted out at the same time as the cannas.

A number of keen growers create canna displays in the shelter of a greenhouse or polytunnel. Planted out in the border soil, with the additional warmth of solar radiation and lack of damage from rain, such shows can be outstanding. The biggest disadvantage is the likely appearance of red spider mite, which can easily decimate plants under cover.

GRANDMOTHER TILLY'S LEGACY

One of the most unusual uses of cannas must the maze created by Maureen and Louis Hankin in Plumsteadville, Pennsylvania. Canna plants lend themselves admirably to such extensive planting and there can be few others that would achieve 1.2m (6ft) in a single season. The 100,000 plants used for the maze are all descended from one type of canna originally grown by 'Grandmother Tilly'. The maze is open to the public during late summer each year.

Because the winters are cold in this area, the plants all have to be lifted each autumn, stored over winter and replanted the next year. Although, probably, one of the most colourful mazes in the world, it must also be one of the most labour-intensive, despite the fact that it doesn't require clipping.

CUT FLOWERS

Nineteenth-century literature refers to the use of cannas as florists' flowers. In my experience cannas make poor cut flowers as the unopened buds do not develop. Did our Victorian forebears know a trick that we have not yet rediscovered?

8

COMMERCIAL PRODUCTION
OF CANNAS

Although most readers will be growing cannas on a garden scale, it may of interest and value to know how the professionals produce them on a large scale for resale. In my research on this subject, I have been assisted by two commercial nurseries in the USA.

QUALITY GLADIOLUS GARDENS

In September 2000, I was privileged to visit the USA on a Canna Study Tour (pp.137–143) and in particular to visit Kent Kelly, who owns and operates a wholesale canna nursery in Jonesboro, Arkansas. The nursery is called Quality Gladiolus Gardens, which is somewhat confusing, as the nursery now specializes in cannas; gladioli and other bulbs now form a very minor part of their business. Because of the long-standing nature of the business, they have chosen to keep their established name.

At Quality Gladiolus Gardens I was able to see, first-hand, the production of cannas on a large commercial scale. Here, about 70 acres of land are used to produce approximately 1.2 million saleable canna rhizomes. Thirty-five cultivars are currently produced, although there are around seventy others under trial, most from Kent Kelly's own hybridizing programme. His production techniques are worth recording in detail.

CULTIVATION

The soil is prepared by chisel ploughing and disc cultivation. No additional organic matter is added, although the remains of the previous year's foliage will have been incorporated. Sometimes a winter wheat cover crop is grown and incorporated into the soil in the spring. The soil is a light silty loam, which is easy to

remove from the crop at the end of the season. A residual herbicide is used to control grasses.

Planting takes place in April, through to mid-May using a minimum of 4,000 to 5,000 rhizomes per acre. These are taken from the previous year's crop and are generally smaller-sized rhizomes, although Kelly believes in the importance of keeping good planting stock. Planting is only partially mechanized. The planting 'machine' is home-made and consists of a platform mounted on the three-point linkage behind a tractor. Under the platform are two coulters, which open shallow furrows. Two members of staff sit on the platform, feeding the rhizomes into the open trench. A set of disc tillers at the rear close the furrow. The nursery has two of these machines.

The nutrition given is determined after soil analysis has been carried out, although the emphasis is on potash and phosphate levels. Nitrogen is only applied as a side dressing later, on the basis that if used at planting, it will have leached before it is of value. There are usually two dressings, one in mid- to late June and the second a month later. The optimum pH is just below 7.0. Micronutrients may occasionally be applied according to analysis.

Weed control is by hand and cultivation. Even on this large scale, hand hoeing takes place between the plants, although between the rows this is carried out mechanically. The crop is rigorously 'rogued' to remove any plants that are not true to type or show signs of disease. During the summer months it is irrigated, as necessary, from a two-acre reservoir fed from a borehole. It is estimated that soil temperatures may reach 40°C (104°F) in the height of summer. On my visit, it was interesting to observe one field of late-planted cannas

One of Kent Kelly's fields of new hybrids being evaluated in their second year of selection.

that had received no irrigation. Although the plants were smaller than the rest, they had survived and were giving a reasonable display, but no doubt the yield from this field would be low.

HARVEST

Harvesting commences at around the beginning of October, by cutting back the top-growth with an agricultural silage harvester. Approximately 7.5cm (3in) of top-growth is left to help avoid damage to the rhizome. The rhizomes are then lifted with a modified potato harvester and channelled into bulk bins that have open, slatted timber sides. These bins are used throughout the harvesting and storage process. They are based on the size of a standard pallet, but are collapsible for summer storage. The aim is to complete digging by the

end of October. There are often several different cultivars in a field and each will be harvested in several batches. This means that if the harvesting process is halted because of bad weather, at least some of each cultivar will have been recovered.

SORTING AND SALE

Once under cover, the roots are washed using a pressurised washing machine: they are taken along a conveyor belt where jets of water remove all the adhering soil. They then go back into the bins for forced air-drying in a modified gas-fired grain dryer. This takes between 4–6 hours at between 12–16°C (55–60°F). The winter storage temperature is between 10–12°C (50–55°F) and humidity is naturally high. It is understood that there is a higher prevalence of storage rots at lower temperatures.

Cleaning and processing begins in early November and usually is completed by early March. Trimming, dividing and grading is done by hand. The plants are graded into two saleable sizes: 2–3 eye divisions, which make up 85 per cent of the sales and 3–5 eye divisions. The different sizes are placed on two conveyor belts, which again drop the stock back into bulk bins. Any damaged or small rhizomes are retained for replanting next year. Most planting stock comes from saving about 15 per cent of the initial harvest.

Designed for minimum fatigue on operatives, the dividing benches are simple constructions with a large hole in the centre to drop rubbish straight through to waste bins. It is estimated that it requires eight staff working until the end of December before there is sufficient stock of each cultivar to commence dispatch.

Most of the sales are wholesale, although limited retailing does exist. Large quantities are despatched in open-meshed plastic crates, although some orders are sent in waxed cardboard boxes. All cannas are packed in peat to prevent moisture-loss and provide handling protection.

HORN CANNA FARM

I am also indebted to Jolene Snow of the Horn Canna Farm in Oklahoma for describing her production techniques. It is interesting to see how they compare with those of Kent Kelly.

Horn Canna Farm was started by John and Frances Horn in the early 1920s with six cannas sent by an aunt in Arkansas. The business was sold on to their eldest son, Neil, in the late 1920s. He sold cannas in surrounding towns and distributed them using a Model T Ford. The farm now produces over three million cannas each year on 130 acres. The cannas are sold throughout the USA and also overseas. Jolene comments that many of the techniques are the same as those used by several generations in this family business. 'We do it this way because it's the way Daddy did it!'

The soil is a light sandy loam which easily washes from the roots in the autumn before the plants are graded and despatched. This must be enriched with organic matter to make it fertile enough to grow cannas. Cannas prefer a neutral soil and lime is rarely used as cannas will not tolerate an alkaline soil. The soil is deeply ploughed to about 30cm (12in) and then broken down to a rough tilth with 'discs' and a harrow. A base dressing of a fertilizer high in phosphates is

A commercial crop of cannas makes an impressive sight in the late summer sunshine.

applied and a residual herbicide to control weeds. On Horn's scale, hand or mechanical weeding is not viable.

In Oklahoma, the dormant canna rhizomes are planted at the end of March and beginning of April. The planting stock consists of small or damaged rhizomes that are not saleable. If there is insufficient of this type of stock, then top-grade rhizomes will be used to ensure that there is sufficient stock for next year.

Planting is partially mechanized. A modified farm implement opens up four small furrows in the soil. On top of this 'plough', a platform holds four people who drop the rhizomes into chutes, which channel them

water, depending on rainfall and temperatures. No additional fertilizer is used. In this commercial situation, flowering and plant height are of little importance but the production of good-sized rhizomes for next year is paramount. Throughout the season the fields are regularly 'rogued', removing or marking stray cultivars to ensure that, when harvested, the crop is pure and to name. This is vital in maintaining a good reputation!

Harvesting begins in October with the removal of the top-growth. As at Quality Gladiolus Gardens, this is done with a modified silage harvester, which cuts the tops, shreds them and blows them back onto the surface between the rows to dry up and eventually be ploughed back in. A further machine cuts the remaining stalks shorter, as excess stalk takes up unnecessary space in winter storage.

Again, similar to Quality Gladiolus Gardens, the rhizomes are then lifted with an adapted potato lifter. The blade goes under two rows at a time and the roots pass up over a chain conveyor, shaking off some of the excess soil. They are then taken by a trailer to the washing barn, where high pressure water removes surplus soil and blowers dry them. From there, they pass along a conveyor belt where staff separate the clumps into '3–5 eye bulbs'. This initial harvesting takes about 30–40 days and brings the crop safely under cover before the bad weather.

Over the winter the crop is re-washed to remove any remaining soil. The old stalks are removed and small 'bulbs' are graded out for replanting. Family members and experienced staff grade and count the stock to ensure high quality. The rhizomes are then stored in peat in wax-lined boxes. This second stage takes a further 60–65 days. The storage barns and cellars are kept at approximately 10°C (50°F). Humidity, which is naturally high from the moisture in the rhizomes, is important to prevent shrivelling.

The sale stock is shipped between November and the beginning of May. Horns sell 50 per cent of their stock to bulb distributors and most of the remainder to garden centres and nurseries. Only about 2–3 per cent goes direct to the home gardener.

From this it can be seen that techniques vary slightly from one producer to another and in different climates; however, the basis of the regime is similar, giving the general principles of commercial production of cannas.

into the open furrows. The furrows are then covered with soil as the implement passes on. The timing of dropping the rhizomes is critical to achieve a spacing of 15–20cm (6–9in). This spacing is much closer than would be used for garden planting because it is based on small rhizomes, some of which may not grow. A soil fungicide is also applied into the furrow before it is closed to reduce rotting of any rhizomes that are bruised or damaged. The planting depth is about 5–7.5cm (2–3in). Again, this is much shallower than is often recommended but deeper planting means that the shoots take longer to emerge: the plant is therefore weaker and flowers later.

During the growing season, the crop is irrigated on a weekly basis with between 2.5 and 5cm (1–2in) of

PLATE VIII

RED-FLOWERED CANNAS

'Assaut'

'Furst Weid'

'Emblème'

'Roi Soleil'

'Black Knight'

'Declaration'

'Brandywine'

'Wintzer's Colossal'

'H.W. Cole'

'President'

'Pfitzer's Cherry Red'

'Strasbourg'

All flowers are shown at approximately half lifesize

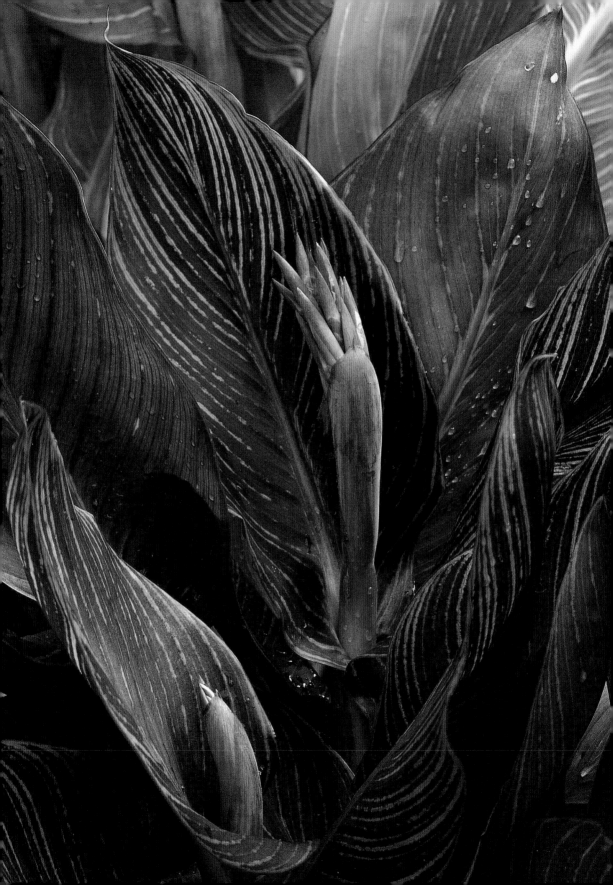

9

CANNA HYBRIDIZATION

Most enthusiasts for a plant will eventually want to try breeding new and improved versions and there is no exception with cannas. From the nineteenth century there has been a succession of both professional and amateur plant breeders who have striven to create the perfect canna. One amateur hybridist I know says that it is his ambition to produce cannas of such brilliance that 'the bees would have to wear sunglasses!'

There is little in historic literature on the genetics of cannas or the practicalities of breeding. However, in *The Canna and How to Grow It* (p.18), Ravenscroft gives practical advice on 'cross-breeding'. He recommends using a camel-hair brush for transferring pollen, and suggests that bright, dry conditions would be ideal for this work. He feels that cross-pollination by insects is unlikely, although he does recommend the removal of unwanted pollen sacs to avoid contamination. Such basic practical advice is still valid, although there may be more involvement from pollinating insects than he supposed.

Current literature has not been much more profitable and the only detailed genetic studies I have discovered originate in India. The following information is drawn from that study and the experience and knowledge of some of the current and recent hybridists.

SELECTION

In trying to achieve improvement or maybe perfection, it is important to know what characteristics would be

Growing to no more than knee-height, 'Pink Sunburst' is the shortest of the foliage cannas.

desirable. The following is a range of model characteristics, although there may be others.

Height

The height of cultivated canna plants has become progressively important and the dwarf cultivars of the late twentieth century, at less than 45cm (18in), bear little resemblance to the tall and unwieldy but 'improved' cannas that Année produced in the mid-nineteenth century (p.11). Out of this list of desirable characteristics, height is probably the one that is presently most important. Modern plant breeders are increasingly looking for compact plants that are not only suitable for smaller gardens but are also very saleable as potted specimens from garden centres.

Hardiness

Obviously this is of far greater importance for plants to be grown in temperate climates. Although it is unlikely that a canna will be developed that is totally frost hardy, undoubtedly there are continuing improvements in the ability to tolerate low temperatures and still perform well.

High Temperature Tolerance

The converse of hardiness, this is of little relevance to those who garden in cooler climates but of great importance to those in the southern states of the USA and other countries, where temperatures may readily exceed 40°C (104°F) for several weeks each summer.

Quantity of Flower

The hybridist is looking for an abundance of flowers, regularly and freely produced. This characteristic is linked with seed sterility, which prevents seed setting and hence encourages continued flowering.

Early Flowering

Ideally, for commercial reasons, a plant should be in flower while in its pot in the garden centre.

Large Flowers

Whereas the flower diameter of the species is generally around 5–7.5cm (2–3in), improvement by breeding has increased it to as much as 10–20cm (4–8in) in many cannas. Both length and breadth of the staminodes has been increased. Although it seems unlikely that major increases in flower size would be either possible or desirable, in general a large flower is an attractive characteristic.

Diversity of Colour

Within existing cannas there is already a wide range of the basic colours, although there are always refinements and combinations that bring a freshness to new cultivars. For many years hybridists have sought to produce a pure white canna and, as the colour white does exist in the species C. liliiflora, this would still seem to be possible. The creation of a blue canna would seem to be unlikely by natural means but not impossible.

Floral Markings

Some of the most beautiful traditional cannas have either spotted, blotched or otherwise marked flowers. Recent breeding has not pursued this and it would seem likely that this could be a future possibility.

Form of Flower

Generally a fuller flower, where the petals overlap giving an almost circular effect, is regarded as desirable. However, a recent trend is to produce some more delicate types with an open, spidery shape. 'Panache' is an example. These flowers are also smaller than most modern hybrids.

Self-cleaning

The ability to drop the dead flowers cleanly from the flower head as they fade is valuable. Not only is the overall effect tidier, but there is less chance of moulds, such as botrytis, developing. This is also linked with the inability to set seed.

Spikes well above Foliage

The flowers should not be masked by the foliage but should stand clear. With heavy, upright foliage this is particularly important. However, it is equally important not to create a 'lollipop' effect.

Form of the Inflorescence

If at all possible, flowers should be borne all round the spike rather than on one side, and the flowers should be well held on the stem at an angle for clear presentation. The overall flower head should be nicely shaped.

Durability of Flowers

Thicker flower parts usually result in longer-lasting flowers as well as making the texture and colour of the flower more intense.

Attractive Foliage

Good leaves make an important foil for any flower. In Britain cannas with dark foliage are favoured, although this is not so in all countries. Smaller foliage is often preferred, if this makes a compact plant. Currently there is considerable interest in the more flamboyant cannas such as 'Durban', grown primarily for their brilliant foliage. Undoubtedly, we shall see further improvements in this area.

Good Tillering

A habit of growth, whereby side shoots are readily produced from the main rootstock, is needed as this means the plant is likely to produce a greater quantity of flower spikes.

Good Rhizome Production

However many other desirable characteristics a plant may have, it is unlikely to be successful if it does not produce a good, well-formed rhizome for overwintering and division.

Compact Rhizomes

This point is of greater importance for the commercial grower who is concerned with lifting and storing large quantities of rhizomes.

Most serious current canna breeding is concentrating on producing compact plants that are early flowering, have an abundance of flowers, continuity of blooming and are self-cleaning. The more ambitious may also be looking for canna flowers with the elusive white or even blue colourings, double flowers, or scent.

THE ELUSIVE WHITE CANNA

Like the highly desired, elusive 'blue' rose, canna hybridists have for years been trying to achieve a white canna. So far, all of those that are described as 'white' are pale primrose or, at the most, open yellow and bleach to an ivory-white in full sun. When placed alongside other truly white flowers, they can be disappointing, although as part of the spectrum of canna colours, they add a useful lightness.

One of the earliest 'whites' is 'Eureka'. It was raised in 1918 and is now considered quite inferior. There is also 'Ambassadour' (not to be confused with 'Ambassador', which is red), 'Ermine', one of the North Star range, 'Begonia' and 'Elaine Gallow'. The recently introduced 'Gran Canaria', which is raised from micro-propagated stock, is listed as a light yellow but ranks highly against all the other so-called whites.

It is likely to be one of those topics that canna aficionados will discuss for some while yet, unless there is a major breakthrough leading to the production of a pure white canna.

GENETICS

In their detailed study entitled 'Evolution of Cultivated Cannas' (see also p.57), Khoshoo and Guha outline their genetic and breeding research. They also refer to an earlier work by Honing who identified 25 different genes controlling a number of basic characteristics. Much of their work is only of academic interest but some reveals the complexity of plant genetics.

Most of the so-called 'white' cannas are really in yellow shades, such as this pale primrose-yellow, fading to ivory.

A Anthocyanin pigment for red flower colour

B and C Red leaf margin

D, E and F Intensification of the effect of A and R

G Extensification of anthocyanin (red colouring) in leaves

H and I Deep yellow plastids

J Deeper vein coloration

K and L Wax layer on leaves

M, N and O Third staminode

P Extensification of central red colour in yellow border

Q Lethal

R Red patches in yellow flowers

S Red flaking on yellow background

T1 to T3 Balanced lethal genes, linked with S

U Lethal in recessive conditions

V Red leaf margin

W Inhibitor for purple

It can be immediately seen that the list is incomplete: there are many characteristics, such as height and control of flowering, that are not identified.

It could be suggested that plant breeding is evolution under the direction of man. With cannas the 'evolution' of cultivated types took place under the temper-

The mutant nature of 'Cleopatra' is demonstrated by the red petals within the yellow flowers.

ate environment of Europe, far away from the tropical and subtropical climates that formed their native habitat. In itself, such a change in habitat may have induced considerable modification in the genetic system of the original species. This is particularly likely to have happened during the extensive hybridization that took place in the late nineteenth century, when species that would not naturally have occurred together were used.

Khoshoo and Guha make particular reference to triploid cultivars. Genetically, such cultivars have three sets of chromosomes rather than two. This may occur in plant breeding without the breeder being aware, although the results are often favourable. It is suggested that as many as 14 per cent of canna cultivars are triploids. Well-known triploid cultivars include 'Black Knight', 'President', 'Louis Cayeux', 'King Humbert', 'Rosemond Coles' and 'Wintzer's Colossal'. Many of these have characteristically very large flowers.

POLLINATION

Canna pollen is quite heavy so there is little likelihood of wind pollination of the flowers; bees and other insects are the main agents for natural pollination. When a canna flower develops, the pollen and the ovule mature at roughly the same time, which means that self-pollination is feasible. This would seem to be quite normal although cross-pollination is equally so. The wild-species cannas have quite small flowers and may, therefore, be less attractive to pollinating insects so self-fertilization may ensure fairly pure communities. The isolation of a single species in the wild will also ensure its pure breeding status. Some canna cultivars, for example 'The President', are sterile and this fact can often be recognized by the stigma, which is thick and blunt or misshapen. The fertile types usually have a narrow, pointed style. Soon after fertilization, the flower dies and the ovary starts to swell.

In hybridization, in order to prevent natural pollination, it is necessary to dissect the flower of the intended seed parent about three days before it would have opened naturally, emasculate the flowers and bag the flower to prevent stray pollination. This is then pollinated manually, two to three days later. It is also useful to bag the pollen parent or remove the pollen a day before the flower opens, to avoid the pollen being 'stolen' by bees. Pollen can be collected any time and stored for use later, although many hybridists prefer to carry out pollination in early morning with fresh pollen. A small artist's brush seems to be the favoured tool for this task, together with a small receptacle, such as a bottle cap, to catch dropped pollen.

Some hybridists report that, without emasculation, by the time flowers were fully open, pollination, although not necessarily fertilization, has often taken place. One grower has observed that the pollen is naturally deposited on the style while the bud is still closed. However, the flower is not fertilized by this because the pollen is deposited on the side of the style, not on the receptive stigma, which is at the tip. By the time the flower opens, the male parts are usually dry and withered. Pollen must then be transferred from the side of the style to the tip. Such a mechanism encourages cross-pollination under natural circumstances. Under conditions where controlled breeding is required, it would seem advisable, nevertheless, to use methods to avoid stray pollination.

LINKED CHARACTERISTICS

Some genetic characteristics seem to be linked. For example, the gladiolus-flowered cannas do not exhibit self-cleaning characteristics and, possibly because of this, are more prone to botrytis disease than many cannas. On the other hand, the orchid-flowered cannas generally have good self-cleaning habits; however, in wet or windy conditions, they may shed their flowers rather too quickly. A curious side issue of this is that orchid-flowered types are not so good as seed parents, possibly because the formation of the abscission layer (the layer of tissue that makes the flower shed cleanly) in some ways aborts the seed production. Gladiolus-flowered types produce more and larger seed, which makes them good seed parents (as opposed to pollen parents).

Tallness seems to be a dominant characteristic. Generally, there is little relationship between flower colour and height, although there are very few tall pure pinks. Most of the real dwarf cultivars of less than 60cm (24in) have green foliage. (Note: in any breeding programme, when evaluating the results, care must be taken to identify truly dwarf plants as opposed to weak plants.)

The flower colour yellow seems to be strongly linked with green foliage. There are very few yellow-flowered cannas with bronze foliage and the few that exist, such as 'Sémaphore', have flowers that are orange-yellow rather than a pure colour. The curious chimera 'Cleopatra' also demonstrates this. This cultivar produces red or yellow flowers and green or bronze foliage, or combinations of all these characteristics. Whenever the plant produces a green-leaved shoot, the flowers are invariably yellow, and pure bronze shoots have red flowers. Not surprisingly, none of the 'white' cannas have bronze foliage; most 'whites' are, in fact, very pale yellows.

Within the range of leaf colour, there is variation from the pure deep burgundy (red), through various shades of bronze and brown to green. In addition there are various shades of green, including the distinct glaucous (grey-blue) colouring that is probably originally acquired from C. glauca. It would seem, from breeding programmes, that dark leaf colouring is a recessive characteristic. In any batch of seedlings from both controlled and open-pollinated crosses, there will be a far lower proportion of dark-leaved seedlings than green-leaved types. However, Sonja Mrsich from New Zealand allows uncontrolled open pollination and reports that the majority of her seedlings are dark leaved. Presumably the proportion of dark-leaved parents she uses will have a bearing on this result. At a practical level, dark-leaved cannas produce less seed. Also, in any batch of seedlings, the greatest proportion of dark-leaved plants will produce red or pink flowers with only a small showing of orange flowers.

There is currently much interest in coloured-leaf and variegated cannas. Examples include 'Pretoria', 'Durban' and 'Striped Beauty'. Sadly, most of these seem to be sterile or infertile. It is thought that they originated as mutations ('Durban' is a mutated form of 'Wyoming'), the majority probably from purple-leaved types ('Pretoria' although gold and green has purple stems, midribs and a dark edge to the leaf). 'Pink Sunburst' will produce viable seed, although seedlings are generally green-leaved, but to date none of its offspring have been of value. There are unverified claims that at least some of the wildly coloured leaf forms have been created by artificial means, such as irradiation. There is currently a report of a new canna that has been produced in India with red and white flowers and striped leaves. It is reputed to have originated from an irradiated red form.

In cross-breeding the hybridist seeks to combine a characteristic from one plant with another from a different plant. So, for example, it might be desirable to try to combine the dwarfness of 'Lucifer' with the large flowers of 'Colossal'. Success might be possible in an initial cross, but it is more likely that a series of crosses and back-crosses to one of the parents would be necessary. However, such an ideal may not be possible due to incompatibility or to linked characteristics which, as discussed, make certain combinations impossible. A few cultivars are sterile so their use as a parent is impossible.

TWO HYBRIDISTS
KENT KELLY

At his nursery, Kent Kelly (p.114) does virtually no controlled crosses (ie hand pollination); most of his hybridization is what he calls 'the numbers game'. Kent saves seed from his own selected stock and grows approximately 5,000 seedlings each year. From these he will select possibly 20 to grow on for further assess-

'Apricot Ice' is a prime example of a modern free-flowering canna with self-cleaning capabilities.

ment, from which he would expect to get maybe one or two new cultivars each year. Although this method is haphazard in many ways, Kent does save seed from large blocks of existing stock that show seedlings with certain genetic patterns. He also grows none of the older tall cultivars and so there is considerable control over the parentage.

Seed scarification is done by hand, using pliers to hold the seed against a grinding wheel. These are then sown in small modules in a greenhouse in early spring. They are transplanted to the trials field after the main crop is planted in late May or early June. During the growing and flowering season, Kent and his son Brian observe the seedling crop and mark any promising seedlings for future trial.

The specific qualities Kent is looking for in his breeding programme include many from the earlier list.

They can be summarized as follows:

- Quantity of flower
- Flower heads clear of foliage
- Early flowering
- Self cleaning
- Clean, healthy foliage
- Compact habit
- Upright habit
- Good tillering
- Good rhizome production
- Rhizomes compact for easy lifting

It is worth commenting that many of the plants in Kent's field of seedlings appeared superior to most cannas grown in Britain at the current time. Some seedlings, such as candy-striped apricots and pinks, looked quite distinct, but would not be selected by Kent because they failed to meet other criteria. Kent is looking for certain cultivars to fill gaps in his range and at the moment he is searching for good orange colours.

Looking at many of his introductions, one can see the high standards that he achieves. It is difficult to single out individuals, but some particularly are worth mentioning. The Futurity Series is especially fine with deep shining burgundy-coloured foliage. In particular 'Futurity Red' is as rich as the established cultivar 'Australia' but with a short habit. 'Apricot Ice' and 'Apricot Dream' both have very soft salmon-apricot colouring, a compact habit and are self cleaning. 'Red Wine' and 'Wine and Roses' both have dark foliage and rich wine-red flowers.

REVEREND CURTIS WALLACE

In contrast to the random breeding work of Kent Kelly, it is of interest to look at some of the hybridization techniques of Curtis Wallace, who describes himself as having a 60-year interest in cannas. Wallace's methods are based on precise control of parentage, regulated pollination and very careful record keeping. Because of this, after many years of experimentation, Wallace is able to produce quite predictable results from many crosses.

His work has been concentrated on producing certain clear colours. A dwarf habit and other good characteristics are of importance, but it seems to be the control of colour that is of primary interest to him. He has established that canna genes carry three fundamental colours – red, orange and yellow – and he suggests that, although an infinite range of colours is possible, it is likely that the human eye can discern no more than about 60. He refers to the pure colour as the 'hue', any mix with white as a 'tint' and the addition of any other colour as causing a 'shade'. In order to create a new colour, he proposes selecting a canna that is nearest to the desired hue and controlling its breeding for several generations. Each batch of seedlings is selected for the desired colour and characteristics. At some stage, there may be a mutation that will bring the offspring closer to the desired goal. He also points out that, initially, one does not have to use parents of the same colour. For example, combining lighter tints of red, yellow and orange may well produce a range of pink cannas.

Wallace points out that line breeding, which is what he does, can work towards eliminating the unwanted, while crossing can introduce new characteristics. Once a new and favourable characteristic has been created, line breeding can be used to reinforce this. On occasions it may be valuable to back-cross (pollinate the offspring with one of the parents) to try to reinforce a certain characteristic.

Over many years, Wallace has produced a wide range of self-coloured cannas, all with the epithet 'North Star'. Sadly, very few are in commercial production. At one stage he had five different whites, with 'North Star Ermine' undoubtedly one of the purest of whites in cultivation. Wallace's correspondence shows an interest in the 'cooler' end of the range and he is constantly searching for any 'hint of blue or purple' in a flower, with which he can work.

Despite being very proud of his creations, Wallace acknowledges that different plants respond differently under different conditions and that they would need testing in varying locations. He also admits that ambient conditions will alter the flower colour in a temporary way. Although few of Wallace's cannas have entered the commercial market, his theories make fascinating reading.

SEED STORAGE

For any hybridist, the storage and viability of seed is of the greatest importance. Seed is not ripe until the capsule is brown and brittle and will then be found to contain dark brown, almost black seeds. These should be separated from the capsule and cleaned of dust and insects. If there is any question that the seed is in any way damp, it should be left to dry for a few days, exposed to the air and without artificial heat. It can then be stored in waxed or paper envelopes. As the seed has a hard coat, water loss is not a great problem and the seed will usually remain viable for several years. Larger quantities of seed can be stored in small plastic containers, such as those used for rolls of photographic film. It should go without saying that any seed from a controlled breeding programme must be labelled carefully.

10

CANNAS IN THE BRITISH ISLES

Because of the seasonal nature of cannas and the fact that in many temperate areas they are replanted each year, the information provided in this chapter can only be true at the time of printing. I believe it is likely that visitors will see cannas in these locations, but cannot be absolutely sure that they will be there from year to year.

Over the last 10 years cannas have been rediscovered in Britain. From being almost obscure plants, available in a very limited range and generally regarded as unfashionable, they have now become quite popular and are frequently featured in the gardening press. The current craze for the exotic style (pp.104–105) has been the perfect medium for their renaissance. Strangely, they are popular in private gardens, large and small, but relatively few local authorities have used them in any quantity for public display. This is probably because there is currently a total inability among local authorities to design good bedding schemes.

The National Council for the Conservation of Plants and Gardens (NCCPG) is a charitable organization that promotes the conservation of garden plants. Much of this is done through a vast network of over 600 National Collections held by nurseries, botanic gardens and many knowledgeable amateur gardeners. There are two National Collections of cannas. These are detailed below.

MY COLLECTION

I first started growing cannas in 1981, when I was a young lecturer teaching horticulture at Norwood Hall,

The bright salmon-pink flowers of 'Tirol' are set off by its dark foliage. There are two versions of this cultivar (see p.100).

a small horticultural college in West London. The college had a close bond with the nearby Kew Gardens, through Brian Halliwell, one of the curators, who is now retired. He generously supplied plant material for the gardens at Norwood Hall and at one stage sent us a collection of five cannas: 'Fireside', 'King Midas', 'King Humbert', 'Assaut' and C. *indica*. I recall thinking that, for our simple purposes, this was rather more cultivars than we needed. Little did I know how my interest would grow!

When I moved on to Reading University, I took divisions of these cannas with me for use in the campus displays. In 1986 we added 'Tirol', 'Picasso' and C. *malawiensis* 'Variegata' (correctly 'Pretoria') from the late Richard Constantine. It was sometime then that my love affair with tender perennials and exotic gardening began. I embarked on a vigorous search for additional cannas, starting with the routine sources from bulb nurseries. I added 'Wyoming', 'Perkeo', 'Strasbourg' and 'Black Knight' and, at the time, was delighted with the diversity I had discovered.

Even in 1991, the RHS *Plant Finder* still only listed 18 species and cultivars available from commercial sources. However, approaches to individuals provided me with C. *iridiflora* 'Ehemanii' from Beth Chatto and C. 'Musifolia' from Christopher Lloyd, and I started to discover the generosity of plant lovers worldwide.

In 1991 I approached the NCCPG for the collection to be registered as a National Collection. It consisted of just 24 cultivars and species when it was granted National Collection status. The collection moved with my job and briefly resided with me at Ascott, a National Trust property. I well recall a late autumn day, driving a heavily laden van full of wet clumps of cannas

PLATE IX

BICOLOURED CANNAS

'Rosemond Coles'

'Lucifer'

'Cleopatre'

'En Avant'

All flowers are shown at approximately half lifesize

'Königin Charlotte'

'Journey's End'

'Italia'

'Golden Girl'

'Dondo'

'Liberty Pink Splash'

'Harvest Yellow'

to their new destination. For just one year, the Victorian grandeur of the Venus Garden was the perfect setting for these historic plants.

CORNISH EPISODE

Fulfilling a lifetime's ambition, my family and I moved in 1994 to Cornwall to set up Brockings Exotics, a small nursery business, and it was here that the collection really expanded. Within just a few weeks of moving, I was presented with an amazing 43 named cultivars from a French grower and 50 cultivars, dubiously named, from an individual collector, who had travelled the world in search of cannas. Over the six years that Brockings ran, I was constantly amazed by people's generosity in sending me unusual cannas for the collection, but also in the sure knowledge that I would sell them through the nursery. I have always stoically defended the sale of surplus plants from the collection, on the basis that good plants should be widely distributed. I also feel that the more people that grow a plant, the less likely it is to be lost – a good conservation practice. Last but by no means least, growing a collection is a costly exercise and the sale of surplus plants has always been an essential cost-covering exercise rather than a profit maker.

MOVING ON

It eventually became evident that despite the very distinct reputation that Brockings had for tender perennials and cannas in particular, it was too small a niche to feed a family. And so, in 1994, I became Grounds Manager at Nottingham University and the collection moved to Nottingham. The cannas have now been displayed on the university campus for four seasons. Initial reservations that cannas would not thrive in the Midlands have proved unfounded. The Trent Valley seems to have a moderate climate with quite hot and sometimes dry summers, coupled with amazingly mild winters. Wide borders backed by high brick walls in the old walled garden of Highfields House are ideal for these plants.

MODERN COLLECTING

Access to the Internet has revolutionized the exchange of information in horticulture is no exception. In recent years, many valuable links have been forged with growers and collectors worldwide. This has led to

plant exchanges with the USA, New Zealand, Malaysia, Thailand and Venezuela. Such exchanges have necessitated coming to grips with the complex and demanding protocol of the Plant Health Regulations and Phytosanitary Certificates, all essential for legal plant exchange across the continents (see p.151).

The naming of plants received from the far side of the world is just as complex. Sometimes they can be

distinct, with properly validated names, which is a relief; however, they can often appear to be identical to existing accessions. Whether these are just misnaming or whether they have been derived from distinct genetic material requires careful assessment.

My links with growers within the British Isles have also continued, and I have found that there is still a genuine desire to share unusual plants. At the moment,

Cannas respond well to the mild climate of Ventnor Botanic Garden (p.134) on the Isle of Wight.

a duplicate collection is being built up by Keith and Christine Hayward (p.134) and such an exercise gives us both an important 'insurance' in the event of losses. Their plants have now been awarded the well-deserved status of a National Collection.

HERE AND NOW

My collection currently numbers about 250 accessions. Records are kept on a computer database and photo-graphs of the plants have been taken over the years. With the advent of digital photography and transparency scanning, the photographs can now be kept alongside the database records. Attempts have been made to verify colours alongside the Royal Horticultural Society colour charts but this has proved complex. Firstly, the colour varies according to the maturity of the flower. Secondly, the observation of the colour is to an extent subjective and dependent on current light conditions, with colours appearing different in bright sunshine and shade. Artificially created shade also affects the flower colour according to the hue of the shade material.

In holding such a collection, there is always a dilemma in knowing what to keep. It is tempting to dispose of poor cultivars, that have been superseded by better, more modern ones. However, in such a reference collection, it is important to retain the widest range of plant material possible for both future information and as a gene bank.

Information on access to my collection may be found in the NCCPG's National Collections Directory.

KEITH HAYWARD'S GARDEN

Keith and Christine Hayward have the second National Collection of cannas. Their collection is 'twinned' with mine for conservation purposes. Each summer they plant out many hundreds of cannas in their small private garden, producing a feast of colour.

The garden is open by private arrangement and they also hold an open weekend each summer. They are located at 25–27 Guildford Road West, Farnborough, GU14 6PS. Information on their open days can be found in the NCCPG's National Collections Directory, which is published annually.

GREAT DIXTER

This lovely traditional garden is the work of Christopher Lloyd, who includes cannas in many of his start-ling planting schemes. In 1993 the old rose garden was revamped as an exotic garden to the shock of the gardening traditionalists. Among a riot of exotic plants, there is a liberal selection of well-grown cannas, including 'Durban', 'Pretoria', 'Louis Cayeux' and 'Wyoming'. The whole garden is a haze of *Verbena bonariensis*. Christopher Lloyd does not have rigid views about colour schemes and some of his plant associations are shockingly effective. The orange-flowered, bronze-leaved 'Wyoming', seen through the pink-purple verbena and intertwined with two-tone orange *Mina lobata*, is an electric fusion that stays in my mind.

In Great Dixter's huge mixed border, cannas are used in big, bold groups with herbaceous perennials, shrubs and annuals. Purple-leaved cannas feature with red hot pokers and native teasels.

Great Dixter is open most afternoons from April to October. It is located near Northiam, 19km (12 miles) north of Hastings, Sussex.

WISLEY GARDEN

This vast garden is owned and maintained by the Royal Horticultural Society. During recent years cannas have increasingly been seen in various parts of the garden. The tradition for an exotic border was started by Ray Waite some years ago and this popular feature has now moved to a more accessible area near the model gardens. Many cannas are featured. The vast herbaceous borders either side of the Long Walk have recently included cannas such as 'Pretoria', 'Durban', 'President' and *C. iridiflora* 'Ehemanii'. Within the greenhouses can be found another splendid clump of *C. iridiflora* 'Ehemanii' and in the summer months water cannas grow in a tropical pool. Outside the greenhouses and just beyond the cactus house is a border permanently planted with cannas. Although now desperately in need of dividing, their vigour shows how cannas can survive outside with just a minimum of protection. The light sandy soil together with the 'stolen' heat from the adjacent greenhouse provides just enough shelter.

In 2002, the RHS will be hosting a trial of cannas in their trial grounds at Wisley. Such trials are aimed at evaluating stocks of commonly available plants for garden usage, and awards are made to the plants that perform best under conditions in the British Isles. Such trials also attempt to sort out problems of nomenclature. Although the results of these trials will be too late for inclusion in this book, hopefully their findings will do much to evaluate cannas today.

Wisley can be found just off the A3, 7m (11km) from Guildford, and is open throughout the year.

VENTNOR BOTANIC GARDENS

This small but exciting botanic garden with a horticultural flavour contains a fascinating range of plants adapted to the mild coastal climate. Cannas can be found in some of the mixed borders and particularly in the walled garden. There is also an exotic garden just inside the entrance area with a vast border of cannas.

Ventnor is on Undercliff Road, Ventnor on the Isle of Wight and is open daily.

OSBORNE HOUSE

This stately home, also on the Isle of Wight, was one of the homes of Queen Victoria. In recent years, the formal bedding on the terrace has been restored with particular emphasis placed on using cultivars available in the late nineteenth century. Cannas are usually included. The recently restored walled garden also includes displays of cannas.

Osborne House is in East Cowes, Isle of Wight, and is open daily in summer.

COTSWOLD WILDLIFE PARK

Alongside the animals in this tourist attraction are spectacular summer displays of exotic plantings, including many cannas.

Cotswold Wildlife Park is in Burford near Oxford and is open daily except Christmas Day.

BRISTOL ZOOLOGICAL GARDENS

This little horticultural time capsule, almost in the centre of Bristol, contains many examples of horticultural excellence. Within the traditional bedding displays, there are often many well-grown cannas, and this is one of the few places the Victorian trick of interplanting cannas with gladiolus can be seen.

The garden is in Downs Road, Clifton, Bristol and is open most days.

EAST RUSTON OLD VICARAGE

Undoubtedly one of the most impressive gardens to be created in the late twentieth century in Britain, this has many different garden 'rooms', all of individual style, including a long tropical border with many cannas among other exotics. Cannas may be found in other areas, such as the walled garden and the Dutch garden. Water cannas are grown in a tank in the conservatory.

Cannas provide a strong accent among annual bedding at Osborne House on the Isle of Wight.

The garden is in East Ruston, near Norwich, Norfolk and is open by arrangement.

WILL GILES' GARDEN

Tucked away in the Norwich suburbs is an amazing pseudo-tropical oasis full of towering bananas, tree ferns, palms and, of course, cannas. This is probably the most exceptional exotic garden in Britain and is well worth a visit during August or early September.

Located at 6 Cotman road, Thorpe, Norwich, the garden is open by arrangement. See the website for dates: www.exoticgarden.com

11

CANNAS IN THE USA

There are many keen amateur growers, collectors and hybridists in many parts of the USA, as well as large wholesale producers. Much of the climate is, of course, temperate and plants need to be grown in very similar ways to the British Isles. In the USA, plants can be left dormant in the ground to over-winter in most areas that are rated USDA Zone 8 and higher. In particular, cannas can usually been seen in the many displays at Brooklyn Botanic Gardens in New York and at Longwood Gardens in Philadelphia. There is also a good collection at Rivendell Botanic Garden, which is located near to Beardstown, Illinois. The garden is not open to the public so, for a visit, contact Stan Tyson, well in advance, by mail or email: rivendellbg@hotmail.com.

CANNA STUDY TOUR TO USA

In September 2000 I was privileged to make a study tour to the USA to visit canna growers, collectors and nurseries. This was sponsored by the RHS and The Stanley Smith Horticultural Trust. The project developed as a result of several years' correspondence with various canna growers, none of whom I had met before.

LONGWOOD GARDENS

My first visit was to Longwood Gardens, America's premier horticultural display gardens: these were established by industrialist Pierre S. du Pont (and are sometimes referred to as the Du Pont Gardens) and offer 425 hectares (1,050 acres) of gardens, including 20 indoor gardens in 1.6 hectares (4 acres) of heated greenhouses. Longwood was created between about 1907 and 1930 and was gifted to the nation as the Longwood Foundation in 1946.

Cannas are of particular interest at Longwood. In the 1970s the water cannas were produced here by crossing *C. glauca* with terrestrial types. Bob Armstrong, now retired, was responsible for these crosses, as well as a subsequent set of hybrids, known as the Longwood Cannas, which were particularly bred to be long-flowering and self-cleaning.

Cannas are used both in the outdoor beds and planters and in magnificent conservatory displays. When I visited, they contributed a major part to the many well-planned summer plantings. As well as the Longwood hybrids, 'Black Knight', 'Phil's Scarlet Lady', 'Tropicanna'™, 'Mrs Du Pont' and others were also planted. Many of the colour schemes were quite adventurous and I particularly recall a fascinating contrast between 'Black Knight' and the purple pods of the hyacinth bean *Dolicos lablab* 'Ruby Moon'. Another memorable combination included the vividly coloured 'Tropicanna'™ with orange zinnias and the purple-leaved grass *Pennisetum setaceum* 'Rubrum'. There were also splendid plantings of cannas with annuals, herbaceous perennials and shrubs in the Flower Garden Walk, which was arranged with hot colours at one end fading down to pastels at the opposite end. The drifts of 'Chesapeake', a near white, at the far end of one border were quite remarkable.

Canna plants are produced for three separate purposes at Longwood: outdoor planting, conservatory display and sale. The stored rhizomes are given a preliminary clean-up and then divided and boxed up into 'flats' (trays) in peat and perlite with a bottom

'Chesapeake' is one of a new generation of cannas, here seen growing in Longwood Gardens.

'Phil's Scarlet Lady' growing outside Longwood Gardens and making a brilliant display.

heat of about (23°C) 75°F. When new growth has commenced, they are potted up into 12.5cm (5in) pots for outdoor use and 17.5cm (7in) pots for conservatory display. At this stage, further division may take place or several divisions may be put in each pot to achieve a balanced plant. A loam-based growing medium is used. They are grown on in a polytunnel with a temperature of around 10–12°C (50–55°F), occasionally dropping to a minimum of 8°C (45°F).

Planting for both outdoor beds and conservatory display will take place in early June. The display in the conservatories is expected to last until October. The major pest under glass is the two-spotted red spider mite, which is controlled by chemical means. Japanese beetle is a problem on outdoor displays. Canna stock for future years is, where possible, retained from that planted outside, on the basis that there is likely to be less incidence of pest and disease than there would be on greenhouse stock.

After lifting, canna stems are reduced to about 35cm (14in) and packed in peat in open-meshed plastic crates. These are stored under benches in a polytunnel heated to a minimum of 3–4°C (38°F) over winter; temperatures may rise to 10°C (50°F). The rhizomes are watered to keep them damp as necessary, although drainage water from the bench-grown plants above is usually sufficient. No fungicides are used over winter.

The Longwood range of cannas is a substantial improvement on many available in cultivation and well worthwhile trialling under British conditions. I was delighted to be presented with a box of rhizomes, complete with Phytosanitary Certificate, to bring back to England with me.

NAUVOO

The next stage of my trip was hosted by Jim Waddick, a Kansas City-based horticulturist with a particular interest in cannas. Our first visit, after a long drive, was to Nauvoo, a small township on the Mississippi. This is the site of an early nineteenth-century Mormon settlement that is currently being restored. The site is beautifully landscaped and there are many plant collections, including oaks, brugmansias, succulents, scented pelargoniums and cannas, which are used for ornamental display. The grounds and plant collections are managed by Durrell Nelson.

We saw two displays of cannas, one a reserve collection of potted stock and the main display planted in a large field. There are approximately 270 cannas listed in Durrel's canna collection. We were joined that day by Stan Tyson, another collector, and the discussion centred around the problems of naming. Durrell's list indicates the origin of most of his stock, some of which came, by a variety of paths, from my own collection. It is easy to see how problems of poor stock or wrong names, for whatever reason, are perpetuated. For example, 'Munchkin' is the same as 'Kansas City', 'Pacific Beauty' should be called 'Sémaphore', and 'Orchid' is the British name for the older 'City of Portland'.

During my visit, several cultivars were noted as worthy additions to my National Collection – particularly valuable would be 'Effie Cole' (one of the original Australian Cole cultivars), 'Gaiety', 'La Traviata' (one of the Grand Opera Series) and 'Liberty Pink' – and I was able to identify some of my own unnamed acquisitions. We agreed that lists would be exchanged and stock swapped at the appropriate time.

RIVENDELL BOTANIC GARDEN

We bade farewell to Durrel and drove on to see Stan's collection of cannas at Rivendell Botanic Garden, near Beardstown. This private botanical garden has a canna collection of around 200 species and cultivars. It was interesting to see both good and poor stock of the familiar mutation 'Cleopatra' and there was also an intriguing seedling raised by Stan as a hybrid between 'Grande' and C. 'Indica Purpurea'. This has the large leaves of 'Grande' but is compact and has a hint of purple in the foliage. There was also a good form of C. *glauca* from wild collected seed. Other cultivars of

note included 'Princess Di', 'Wine and Roses', 'Tropical Sunrise' and 'Liberty Splash Pink'.

Stan has an exceptional way of storing cannas: the rhizomes are cleaned and divided in the autumn and selected stock is secured in zip-loc plastic bags for frost-free storage. Although it would seem that this closed environment would encourage decay, Stan reports a high level of success.

MISSOURI BOTANIC GARDEN

The following day, Jim Waddick and I drove on to visit Missouri Botanic Garden. Here we were met by Jason Delaney, the Outdoor Horticulturist, whose responsibilities include the bulb garden. The summer displays here include many groups of cannas grown with tender perennials giving much colour in this otherwise traditionally spring-centred garden. There were some good blocks of the seed-raised 'Tropical Rose'.

We then moved to the home-gardening display beds, where there were more cannas and an impressive exotic border. Coming from a chilly climate, I could not but be impressed by the enormous towering leaves

'Effie Cole' seen growing among Durrell Nelson's collection of cannas at Nauvoo near Mississippi.

PLATE X

RECENTLY INTRODUCED CANNAS

'Champigny'

'Brandywine'

'Empire'

'Lippo'

'Penn'

All flowers are shown at approximately half lifesize

'Lenape'

'Maggie'

'Pink Futurity'

'Yellow Futurity'

'Conestoga'

of some of the cannas. Most of the cultivars I saw here had already been observed elsewhere, although the plant associations were good and the plants well grown. It was also useful to verify some names. In the pools near the visitor centre, aquatic cannas such as 'Endeavour' and 'Ra' were also well represented.

On the Saturday morning I lectured to members of the Kansas City Garden Centre Association firstly on 'Cannas' and then 'Tender Perennials'. Both talks were well received and much interest expressed in cannas.

On the Sunday we took a visit to the Powell Gardens, a new botanical garden on a 370-hectare (915-acre) site, 30 miles east of Kansas City. Much of the site is still incomplete, as work only commenced in 1988; however, around the visitor centre there are extensive display beds, which, during my visit, included fine groups of cannas among exotic plantings. Many of the cultivars were familiar but, again, it was useful to record good imaginative associations produced on a large

scale. The cultivar 'Orange Punch' was one that I had not seen before.

The weekend finished with a brief circuit of Jim's own garden. Cannas in Jim's collection were unique for the amount of growth they had made despite an exceedingly hot and dry summer. Most were well over 1.8m (6ft). Amazingly, the variegated 'Stuttgart', which in Britain is normally never without scorch, was almost perfect. A number of new cultivars were noted and names discussed.

QUALITY GLADIOLUS GARDENS
The next stage of my trip took me via Dallas and Memphis to Arkansas in order to visit Kent Kelly, who owns the wholesale canna nursery Quality Gladiolus Gardens discussed in chapter 8 (pp.114–119).

This was a very valuable part of my trip as I was able to see cannas produced on a large commercial scale and to see hybridization in practice. Kent proved to be most willing to discuss his techniques with me and also had a valuable archive of material from other hybridizers and nurserymen. About 28.5 hectares (70 acres) of

Cannas, such as 'Conestoga' shown here, are also grown as conservatory plants at Longwood Gardens.

land are used to grow approximately 1.2 million canna rhizomes. Thirty-five cultivars are currently produced, although there are around 70 others under trial, many of Kent's own raising. This visit was also exceedingly valuable in acquiring third-party information as Kent has corresponded with a number of other growers and hybridists, including the late Mrs Sarver (p.21) and Reverend Curtis Wallace (p.127).

OLD HOUSE GARDENS AND
MIKE UNDERWOOD

Finally, I flew on via Chicago to Detroit to visit Scott Kunst, who runs a bulb company called Old House Gardens, specializing in 'heirloom bulbs'. It was through our correspondence on old cannas that we became acquainted some years ago. Scott lists 17 nineteenth-century cannas in his catalogue and most were displayed around his house, together with old dahlias, caladiums, crinums and colocasias.

The next day I gave two more lectures, this time to The Michigan Hardy Plant Society. After lunch, Scott and I drove out to beyond St Johns to the home of Mike Underwood, another canna collector. Mike lives in an old wooden farmhouse surrounded by goats, sheep, miniature horses, geese, emus and, of course, cannas! We were soon deep in discussion on the inexhaustible subject of naming. Mike's collection numbers just on 100, not surprisingly mainly cultivars. Many plants were familiar and had, inevitably, come through exchanges with the other collectors, whom I had already seen. There were, however, some unique names such as C. 'Gladiflora', which, if true to type, is another nineteenth-century cultivar. It was interesting to see 'North Star Red', one of the Curtis Wallace hybrids. Mike had a range of small-flowered seedlings, presumably from crosses with C. *glauca* as they displayed the narrow glaucous leaf. I was pleased to receive seed from these as I would like to pursue the breeding of a range of more delicate cannas such as 'Panache'.

MICHIGAN STATE UNIVERSITY
AND COOLEY GARDENS

On the Saturday morning, I presented the last of my lectures at Michigan State University, as part of their programme for home gardeners. Once again, the response was very warm: in fact, the lecture became almost informal with the audience both asking question and contributing. We were then shown some of the impressive display gardens around the campus area, including a small collection of cannas. There are some impressive bedding displays using bold groups of cannas and other exotics.

The afternoon was finished at the nearby Cooley Gardens, in the company of Eric Stenson, the director. This small public garden retains the intimate atmosphere of a large private garden, but it is large enough to attract many visitors. There are several areas, each with a different ambience, and cannas were used in many different schemes. The bedding schemes were formal and impressive but contained a wide range of plants and colours, skilfully combined. Cannas including 'Tropicanna'™, 'Louis Cottin' and 'Futurity Red' were well represented.

On the Sunday, in the company of Mike Underwood, we returned to Ann Arbour, via Saugur Nurseries, a rural plantsman's paradise with rambling garden and sales areas stretching in every direction. I was delighted to obtain canna 'Red Futurity', which I had admired in many places.

Over a two-week period I was able to see both impressive canna collections and magnificent displays of cannas. It was most valuable to be able to verify a number of naming problems and to gather information. I was most impressed by some of the new cultivars available in the USA and I look forward to acquiring these for trial in Britain. Finally, it was encouraging to see how widely cannas are now grown in the USA and the imaginative ways in which they are grouped with other plants.

12

CANNAS WORLDWIDE

There are many other countries throughout the world where cannas are grown. The following are brief descriptions of those links that I have made; I am well aware that there may be many other collections that, as yet, I have not discovered.

AUSTRALIA

Cannas are found in almost every garden in Australia. One of the reasons why they are so widely grown is because the climate allows them to be grown without annual lifting. Indeed, in many areas they grow and flower continuously, although in Melbourne they go dormant for some months each year. Because they are easy to cultivate, they are often regarded as fillers for odd corners, providing a certain level of showiness for a minimum of attention. There are a few, very common cultivars that appear everywhere and many gardeners merely mow them down once a year for tidiness.

Quite a few large parks have big display beds. There is a collection at Melbourne Botanical Gardens. It was first established in 1949 but does not seem to have been developed in recent years. Another good display is found in The Queen Victoria Gardens in Bendigo and includes a number of the Cole cultivars. The Ornamental Plant Collections Association in Australia (OPCA) have been working with the staff from both of these gardens to try to verify the naming of these plants, but the project seems to have been shelved due to the inability to finalize naming.

Cannas are rarely found in Australian nurseries, although there are a few growers who do offer them.

'General Eisenhower', worth growing for its foliage alone, also produces orange flowers.

'Tropicanna'™ is widely available. It is not surprising to hear that nomenclature is a problem and buying named cultivars is a chancy business.

FRANCE

Cannas are quite widely grown in France and often seen in bold blocks in municipal plantings. There is a good collection in the botanic garden at Lyon and the French National Collection of Cannas is held by the local parks department at Montpellier in the South of France.

GERMANY

Although cannas are not very popular in Germany, there is said to be a good collection at the Munich Botanic Garden. A group of amateur plantspeople are working together to develop a collection there.

HOLLAND

It is not surprising that cannas are widely grown in Holland as a commercial crop alongside so many other bulbous plants. Sadly, there are reports that virus is widespread among Dutch stocks. Some suppliers also have a bad reputation for wrong naming. This slackness is defended on the basis that most purchasers are interested in colour and not the precise name.

JAPAN

The manager of a botanic garden in Japan comments that C. indica was introduced in 1695 and by the early twentieth century there were lists of over 200 cultivars, which had been introduced from France. Around the time of World War II, they lost favour and many cultivars disappeared. Nowadays, they are more or less

'Pfitzer's Salmon Pink' is a free-flowering, compact cultivar with large green leaves.

ignored in much of Japan, despite the fact that the Pacific Ocean areas have an almost tropical climate.

A few nurseries offer some cultivars, including the seed-raised 'Tropical Rose' and 'Tropical Red' introduced by Takii nursery. Those available mostly have western names, although there are some such as 'Isogahama', 'Hinokoromo' and 'Hatushimo' which are Japanese.

NEW ZEALAND

My main knowledge of cannas in New Zealand is through correspondence with Sonja Mrsich, who grows and sells cannas from her small nursery, Podgora Gardens, in Waipu. It is only a part-time nursery as the family are primarily dairy farmers.

The collection was developed by Sonja Mrsich's parents in the late 1940s and 1950s. Many of the original plants came from R. E. Harrison, a nurseryman of Palmerston North, in 1950. Later plants came from the Singapore Botanic Gardens, including the cultivar 'Singapore Girl', which was named after the girl in the Singapore Airlines advert.

Sonja took over the cannas in the 1970s. The collection again grew, with the addition of about 60 more cultivars, swapped with Bendigo City Council in Australia. Not surprisingly, many were duplicates under different names. In particular they have an extensive list of the Australian Cole cultivars. Other exceptional cultivars are 'Statue of Liberty' and 'Australia'.

In New Zealand, cannas are cut back to the ground in September or October (spring), and dressed with blood and bone fertilizer. A dressing of lime is also sometimes given.

New cultivars are not actively bred but seed is collected from random pollination and grown on. Bumble bees are the most familiar local pollinating agents. Ruthless selection takes place and only distinct improvements are kept. Their introductions include 'Michelle M', 'Katie Mac', 'Lemon Chiffon', 'Black Magic', 'Monet Sunset' and 'Podgora'. As yet these are not widely available.

RUSSIA

The Nikita Botanical Gardens did have a good collection of over 300 cultivars and species, although it is not known whether this is still being developed. As well as many established western cultivars, there was a number of Russian origin such as 'Crimea Riviera', 'Flame of Crimea' and 'Sun's Beauty'.

THAILAND

The Nong Nooch Tropical Garden in Sattahip, Chonuri Province is a vast, privately owned plant collection with large numbers of bromeliads, cacti, palms, heliconias, gingers, bougainvilleas and cannas. The canna collection was only started in 1996 but is being seriously developed by the owner, Kampon Tansacha, and his garden's curator, Michael Ferrero.

The freely-produced flowers of 'Cleopatre' are vivid orange, delicately line with gold.

APPENDICES

APPENDIX 1

GLOSSARY

Acuminate Ending with a long, tapering point. This is an alternative leaf ending found in some cannas.

Acute Ending with a short, sharp point. Generally refers to leaves. Most canna leaves are acute.

Apex Tip or growing point of part of a plant such as a leaf.

Alternate Leaves borne singly at each node on either side of the stem.

Capsule A dry fruit that splits open to disperse the ripe seeds.

Carpel One of the sections of a fruit, holding the seeds. Cannas have three carpels.

Chimera Plant composed of two or more genetically different tissues; resulting from a mutation.

Cultivar A 'cultivated variety'; that is, any plant which has been specifically bred or appeared through cultivation as opposed to occurring naturally within the wild. Many gardeners use the word 'variety' when they mean 'cultivar'. Cultivar names have a capital letter and are contained within single quotes, eg. 'Wyoming'.

Double A flower with multiple petals, more than is found in the normal wild type.

Elliptical In leaves where it is broadest at the centre, tapering to both ends. Length is approximately twice the width.

F$_1$ Hybrid First generation. A vigorous and uniform strain of plants produced from crossing two distinct pure-bred lines. F$_1$ Hybrids do not breed true.

Family Primary category in plant classification, between order and genus. Plants within a family (eg. Cannaceae) have certain common characteristics.

Farina An attractive white floury deposit produced on the stems of some plants, eg. *Canna* 'Black Knight'.

Fertile Able to produce functional pollen or seeds.

Fertilization The sexual fusion of pollen with the ovules, eventually resulting in seed production.

Genus (genera) Primary category of plant classification (eg. *Canna*) Encompasses species that share common characteristics.

Glabrous Smooth and hairless.

Glaucous With a blue-green, blue-grey or silvery whitish hue. Usually refers to the leaves and stems, eg. *C. glauca*.

Hardiness The ability of a plant to withstand adverse conditions. In a temperate climate this usually means low temperatures. More generally used to mean just 'tough' and easy to grow.

Herbaceous plant A non-woody plant that dies back to the ground and becomes dormant at the end of its growing season.

Inflorescence Arrangement of the flowers on a single stem. In cannas this is usually a raceme.

John Innes composts A traditional range of potting composts, based on a mixture of sterilized loam (a type of soil), peat and sand, with added fertilizers and lime.

Labellum (lip) Prominent lower lobe on certain flowers formed from a petal or, in the case of cannas, a staminode. Usually very showy.

Lamina (leaf blade) The flat, thin, often broad part of a leaf, as distinct from the stalk (petiole).

Lanceolate (lance-shaped) Refers to a leaf that is broadest below the centre and tapering to a narrow point. Usually long and thin with the length 3–6 times the width.

Lanuginose Covered with fine hair.

Leaf axil Angle formed between the leaf and stem. Side shoots are usually produced here.

Loam Highly fertile, moisture-retentive soil containing a balanced mix of clay, silt and sand.

Marginal aquatic Plants that require constantly moist

conditions, either at the edge of a water feature or within the shallow water, eg. water cannas.

Midrib The central, raised portion of a leaf. The midrib gives structure to the leaf and transports water and nutrients to the leaf blade. In many cannas it is darker coloured than the rest of the leaf and is an attractive feature of the plant.

Monocotyledon A plant that produces a single seed leaf, has parallel veined leaves and makes no woody tissue. Floral parts are usually in threes. All cannas are monocotyledons.

Nectar Sugary liquid secreted by flowers to attract pollinating agents such as bees.

Node Point on a stem, sometimes swollen, at which leaves, buds and flowers arise.

Organic In gardening terms this refers to practices using only natural and environmentally friendly materials.

Oval Another leaf shape common in cannas. Broadly elliptical, rounded at both ends with slightly parallel sides in the centre. Length ½–2 times the width.

Ovary Female organ of a flower containing ovules.

Panicle Branched raceme, loosely branched inflorescence, eg. *C. iridiflora*.

Parasite Organism that derives nutrients from another host species to the detriment of the latter. There are various beneficial parasites that are used to control plant pests.

Pedicel Stalk of a flower or inflorescence.

Petaloid Similar to a petal in colour, shape and texture. In cannas the stamens are petaloid.

Petiole The stalk that attaches the leaf to the stem. In cannas this is often non-existent or very short.

pH Measure of the acidity or alkalinity of a soil.

Pollen Grains released from the anthers of a flower, containing the male elements essential for fertilization and seed production.

Pollination The transfer of pollen from the anthers to the stigma of a flower. Distinct from fertilization, which is the next stage.

Pulvinus Localized enlargement of the base of a leaf stalk.

Raceme A type of inflorescence or flower head, radiating from a single unbranched stem, the youngest flowers near the tip. Cannas most commonly have racemose inflorescences.

Reflexed Arched or bent sharply back towards the axis. Many cannas have a strongly reflexed lip.

Rhizome A specialized underground stem that is swollen with stored nutrients and helps the plant to survive adverse conditions such as a winter dormant period.

Scarify To scrape or score the outer layers of a seed. A useful practice with cannas, which have a hard seed coat.

Self-coloured A flower with a single, uniform colour.

Self-pollinate Process whereby the pollen from the anthers of a flower reaches the stigma of the same flower or another flower on the same plant.

Sepals Floral parts, jointly referred to as the calyx. Usually green and often insignificant.

Sessile Leaves without a leaf stalk. Cannas are mostly sessile.

Species A basic category in plant classification, ranked below genus and consisting of plants with similar characteristics.

Stamen Male part of the flower consisting of anther usually borne on a filament. In cannas the stamens are modified to look like petals (petaloid staminodes).

Staminode Modified stamen resembling a petal. In cannas these are the showy parts of the flower.

Stigma The fertile female part of the flower that receives the pollen.

Subtropical High temperature zones located between tropical and temperate. Rainfall often as monsoon-type storms. Many cannas come from subtropical areas.

Temperate Climate zones between the subtropics and the polar circles, which experience distinct seasons with some temperature fluctuations. Rainfall occurs throughout the year. Cannas have become adapted to grow in temperate climates.

Tropical Refers to hot climatic zones with a hot, steamy environment that encourages lush growth. Some cannas come from tropical areas.

Tuber An underground swollen root.

Tubercles Small, wart-like projections.

Undulate Wavy, usually referring to the margins of a leaf.

Woody Refers to the ability to produce persistent stems. Although cannas produce stems of some height, these are not woody and will not survive for a prolonged period of time.

APPENDIX 2

WHERE TO BUY CANNAS

There are relatively few nurseries that specialize in cannas. Most are bulb growers and include a selection of cannas as dry rhizomes available during the late winter and spring months. Some growers of unusual plants offer cannas as growing plants later in the season.

BRITISH ISLES

The Canna Company
14 Park Close, Mapperley,
Nottingham, NG3 5FB.
email: ian@cookecannas.co.uk
website: www.cookecannas.co.uk
National Collection Holder, 2 x 1st Class stamps for mail order catalogue. Surplus plants from the National Collection are sold in late spring and summer. Rare and unusual types are available in small quantities. Trading is mainly in growing plants, from £5 each.

Hart Canna
25-27 Guildford Road West,
Farnborough, Hants GU14 6PS.
email:canna@hartcanna.com
website: www.hartcanna.com
This recently established company sprang from an amateur collection. It particularly supplies dry rhizomes in the spring months. A restricted list of readily available types is offered in large quantities. As well as these, there are other collectors' items available in small quantities and some growing plants later in the season. Rhizomes are sold in packs of three, mostly at around £6 for three.

Brian and Heather Hiley
25 Little Woodcote Estate,
Wallington, Surrey.
A well-established nursery offering a wide range of unusual plants, including many tender perennials and cannas. Sold during spring and summer as growing plants.

Parkers Bulbs
452 Chester Road, Old Trafford,
Manchester M16 9HL.
A small selection of cannas as dry rhizomes. One of the few firms to stock 'Pretoria' and 'Cleopatra'. These are available from its spring catalogue, retail and wholesale, along with a wide range of bulbs. Prices are very competitive from the wholesale list.

Peter Nyssen
124 Flixton Road, Urmston,
Manchester M41 5BG.
A small range of popular cannas are offered as dry rhizomes in the spring. Although wholesale suppliers, they will supply down to 10 of each cultivar. Rates are good.

Terence Bloch
9 Colberg Place, Stamford Hill,
London N16 5RA.
The beautifully presented 'Tropical Explorer's Plant Catalogue' includes 20 or so cannas, some of which are quite unusual and originate from the owner's travels in South Africa. Growing plants only in early summer. Many other lovely exotics are also available.

FRANCE
Ets Pierre Turc et Fils
Les Richelets, 49630 Mazé.
email: turc@turcieflor.com
website: www.turcieflor.com
Wholesale growers of bulbs, especially cannas. They will export dormant rhizomes and sell in small quantities. The canna fields are well worth a visit in the summer but be prepared to communicate with this firm in its native language.

Ernest Turc
BP 315-F, 49003, Angers, Cedex 01.
email: turc.bulbes@wanadoo.fr
website: www.turcbulbs.com
Another branch of the family also breeding and growing cannas on a wholesale scale, among many other bulbs. Quite a number of traditional cultivars were raised and registered by Ernest Turc.

USA
Aaron's Amaryllis and Canna Bulb Farm PO Box 800, Sumner, Georgia 31789.
website: www.aaronscanna-amaryllis.com
The website gives a lovely presentation of some splendid-looking cultivars, including some unusual variegated types not offered elsewhere. Some of the names are not familiar, although the plants are! Many of their offerings seem to originate from TyTy Plantations. Prices vary from $8 to an amazing $65.

Brent & Becky's Bulbs

7463 Heath Trail, Gloucester, Virginia 23061.
email: info@brentandbeckysbulbs.com
website: www.brentandbeckysbulbs.com
Brent and Becky Heath have a nice catalogue with a good selection of cannas available and are very pleasant to work with.

Horn Canna Farm

Route 1, Box 94, Carnegie, Oklahoma 73015.
email: cannas@cannas.net
website: www.cannas.net
Claiming to be the world's largest exclusive canna growers, Horn's grow primarily for wholesale but also do a small retail mail-order business. The range is limited but the quality is high. Retail prices are around 12 bulbs for $10 plus tax and shipping charges.

Kelly's Plant World

10266 E Princeton, Sanger, California 93657.
Herb Kelly, a well-established canna collector and breeder, offers a sumptuous range of cannas. His prices are higher than some vendors and he can only be reached by mail.

Louisiana Nursery

5853 Hwy 182, Opelousas, LA 70570.
website: www.durionursery.com
Offers 40 different cannas for sale.

Old House Gardens

536 Third Street, Ann Arbor, Michigan 48103-4957.
email: ohgbulbs@aol.com; website: www.oldhousegardens.com
This firm is owned by Scott Kunst and specializes in 'heirloom bulbs'. The range of cannas is all well authenticated and includes old nineteenth-century cultivars such as 'Florence Vaughan' 1893, 'Sémaphore' 1895 and 'Königin Charlotte' 1892.

Plant Delights Nursery

9241 Sauls Road, Raleigh, NC 27603.
website: www.plantdelights.com
Offers unique selections of canna lillies. Many of the newer introductions are truly stunning. Plants are growing in gallon pots, and not shipped as dry rhizomes.

Plumeria People

PO Box 31668, Houston, Texas 77231-1668.
website: www.plumeriapeople.com
Provide about 20 reasonably priced selections.

Pride of the Plains Bulb Farms

PO Box 394, Olton, Texas 79064.
email: bulbsinc@fivearea.com
This nursery has a list of around 40 or so cannas, including some good modern cultivars.

Quality Gladiolus Gardens

PO Box 458, Jonesboro, Arkansas 72403.
email: canna@inet-direct.com
website: www.qualitycannas.net
This large wholesale grower produces a range of bulbs, but cannas are a speciality. The nursery probably offers the widest range of modern dwarf cannas, many from Kent Kelly's own breeding programme. Although most sales are wholesale, they will supply in retail quantities.

San Marcos Growers

PO Box 6827, Santa Barbara, California 93160.
email: sales@smgrowers.com
website: www.smgrowers.com
Wholesale growers with a good range of cannas, including some of Herb Kelly's introductions such as 'Herb's White'.

Stokes Tropicals

PO Box 9868, New Iberia, LA 70562-9868.
email: gstokes@stokestropicals.com
website: www.stokestropicals.com
Catalogue offers a choice selection of cannas in cold climates.

NEW ZEALAND

Podgora Gardens Sonya Mrsich, Shoemaker Road, PO Box 46, Waipu, North Island.
This small nursery specializes in cannas and its list includes many unique types not readily available elsewhere. This must be one of the 'shrines' for all canna worshippers to visit! Mail order is possible.

AUSTRALIA

Canna Brae Country Garden

Ann Glancy, 35 Felix Crescent, Ringwood, Melbourne, Victoria.
Over 180 cannas are offered by mail order.

Vicki Staal PO Box 99, Palmwood, Queensland.
Over 40 cultivars offered by mail order.

Bernard Yorke 89 Talinga Drive, Park Ridge 4125, Queensland.
email: bsyorke@optusnet.com.au
Canna collector who sells surplus plants. New and unusual cultivars available in small quantities.

APPENDIX 3

CANNAS ON THE WEB

With the widespread availability of computers, the internet has invaded every aspect of society. The world of cannas is no exception and there are websites with useful information as well as specialized internet discussion groups.

DISCUSSION GROUPS

Discussion group members can post messages or questions, which can then be received as emails or viewed on the website. The following are all part of the 'eGroup' network. You can join any group simply by visiting the website.

canna-net

www.egroups.com/group/ canna-net

This group was the first to be started and includes many canna lovers who grow purely for private pleasure. The rules of the group do not allow the posting of pictures.

canna

www.egroups.com/group/canna

This second group grew out of the first and comprises more serious growers and collectors and is distinct in that it allows the posting of pictures, which, of course, is most valuable in the discussion of naming.

ExoticGardeningUK

www.egroups.com/group/Exotic GardeningUK

Although this is a more general group, discussion will include cannas and many plants that are often associated with cannas.

WEBSITES

There are many websites that mention cannas and a few that are dedicated to this genus.

Aaron's Amaryllis and Canna Bulb Farm Nursery

www.aaronscanna-amaryllis.com

This is a well laid-out site that is primarily an on-line catalogue and leads to an ordering page. There are some lovely pictures although the naming of some of the cannas is very doubtful.

Aloha Tropicals

http://alohatropicals.com/can nas.html

A commercial site with a few popular cannas described and illustrated.

Bloemisterij Goeminne

www.goeminne.com/

A wholesale Dutch nursery with some cannas illustrated.

Canna – Hart Canna

www.hartcanna.com

A very informative and well laid-out site. Many cultivars are listed and described, together with cultural information.

Canna Lily Watercolor-Martha Garren

www.pcisys.net/~tailwater/marthas /watrcana.htm

Floridata Canna flaccida

www.floridata.com/ref/c/can n_fla.cfm

A single page with a lovely picture

of this species and a description.

Glasshouse Works

www.glasshouseworks.com

An exotic plant nursery with a colourful website including a few cannas.

Longwood Gardens – Home Page

www.longwoodgardens.org

A general site describing this wonderful garden which is home to the Longwood Cannas.

National Collection of Cannas

www.cookecannas.co.uk

This is my website with detailed pages on history, cultivation and both descriptions and pictures. Some discussion on new cultivars and links to other websites.

Old House Gardens

www.oldhousegardens.com

Specializing in heirloom bulbs, this commercial site describes and offers just a few old cannas.

Plant Delights catalogue

www.plantdel.com

An online catalogue of a few cannas.

TyTy

www.tytyga.com

A commercial nursery site. Established names and new introductions available from their online catalogue, ranging from $25 each for the new introductions to 3 for $1.75 for the 'older varieties'.

APPENDIX 4

IMPORTING AND EXPORTING CANNAS

With the wealth of cannas available worldwide, it is likely that gardeners will want to import some. There may be the temptation to bring back plants from a holiday or to send for plants advertised on nursery websites. Correspondence with other growers will often lead to a plant exchanges.

Plant importing can be both very rewarding and tedious and time consuming. Commercial nurseries that offer an overseas despatch service will know all the procedures but if you are arranging exchanges with other amateurs, then careful preparation should be made. In order to ensure that undesirable pests are not transmitted, strict import and export regulations are in force. Plants travelling without the correct documentation can be seized and destroyed. It is important, therefore, to follow the correct procedures – documentation and some inspection usually has to come from the country of origin.

Cannas are usually best transported to and from overseas while they are dormant. Restrictions on dormant 'bulbs' are less stringent as there is less likelihood of a pathogen being transmitted. If sending in the summer, it is best to cut down all stems and remove all foliage, leaving just the rhizome and any attached roots. Most countries will require the rhizomes to be free from all soil. The rhizomes are then packed in an inert material such as slightly damp perlite or vermiculite. If the roots are totally dormant and dry, no packaging may be necessary. Outer wrapping can be polythene or newspaper. If the plants are likely to be in transit for a long while, plants in polythene can sweat and rot so paper may be preferable. Labelling of plant material is important, and parcels should be wrapped in such a way that they can be opened and inspected without undue trouble. Usually it is necessary to attach copies of the paperwork to the outside of the carton as well as inside. In order to get the plants to their destination in the shortest possible time, it is essential to use air mail or an international courier service.

Imports within the European Community

Within the EC there are relatively few controls provided that plants are visibly free from signs of pests and diseases, they are intended for your personal use and they are carried in your personal luggage. Commercial quantities must be accompanied by a Phytosanitary Certificate. The Euro-Mediterranean area, which includes Algeria, the Canary Islands, Cyprus, Egypt, Israel, Jordan, Lebanon, Libya, Malta, Morocco, Norway, Switzerland, Syria, Tunisia, and Turkey, has some restrictions but personal imports are still allowed – in the case of cannas, up to 2kg (4lb) of dormant rhizomes.

Beyond the EC

To export cannas from the UK, it is important to be sure of the precise regulations of the country they are going to. Plants may require both a Phytosanitary Certificate and an Import Permit. In the UK the Phytosanitary Certificate is obtained from the local Plant Health Office, part of MAFF (Ministry of Agriculture, Food and Fisheries). Their inspector will check the plants that have been prepared for export. They should be ready for their final packaging as the inspector may wish to inspect and then seal the parcel. There is a charge for this service. The Import Permit is issued by the receiving country and would normally be arranged by the recipient and sent to the exporter in advance.

In order to import cannas to the UK, just a Phytosanitary Certificate from the sending country is required. This will enable the plants to pass through customs with the least delay. A copy of the certificate will have been sent to the local Plant Health Inspector in the United Kingdom who will arrange to come and inspect the plants. It is wise to grow all newly imported plants in a separate or isolated location until their health is verified.

Within the USA

In the USA, imports and exports are controlled by APHIS (Animal and Plant Health Inspection Service). Plants coming into the USA must be accompanied by a Phytosanitary Certificate and an Import Permit. The latter includes a yellow and green label directing the plants to the nearest Inspection Station where the plants are examined and if free of pests and diseases, sent on to their final destination.

APPENDIX 5

CREAM-OF-THE-CROP CANNAS

The following lists have been drawn up to help readers select cannas for certain purposes. Inevitably they reflect my opinion and there may be others that could be included.

Historic cultivars

With approximate dates of introduction in brackets. All these cultivars are believed to be available today.

Pre-1900
'Cleopatra' (1895)
'Florence Vaughan' (1893)
'Italia' (1893)
'Königen Charlotte' (1892)
'Prince Charmant' (1892)
'Sémaphore' (1895)
'Shenandoah' (1894)

Early twentieth century
'Centenaire de Rozain-Boucharlat' (1925)
'City of Portland' (1916)
'Emblème' (1927)
'En Avant' (1914)
'Ingeborg' (1916)
'King Humbert' (1902)
'Lafayette' (1925)
'Louis Cayeux' (1924)
'Madame Angele Martin' (1915)
'Madame Paul Casaneuve' (1902)
'Oiseau de Feu' (1911)
'Oiseau d'Or' (1923)
'President' (1923)
'Richard Wallace' (1902)
'Roi Soleil' (1930)
'Stadt Fellbach' (1934)

'Tirol' (1930)
'Wyoming' (1906)

Red flowers and green foliage
'Aloha'
'Bonfire'
'Brilliant'
'Crimson Beauty'
'Declaration'
'Elizabeth Hoss'
'Empire'
'Eric Neubert'
'Firebird'
'Fireside'
'H. W. Cole'
'L'Aiglon'
'Marvel'
'Merle Cole'
'Oiseau de Feu'
'President'
'Roi Soleil'
'Roitelot'
'Strasbourg'
'Valentine'
'Wintzer's Colossal'

Red flowers with dark foliage
'Ambassador'
'America'
'Assaut'
'Black Knight'
'Emblème'
'Etoile du Feu'
'Feuerzauber'
'Hercule'
'King Humbert'
'Lafayette'
'Red Futurity'

'Red Wine'
'Statue of Liberty'
'Wine 'n Roses'

Orange flowers with green foliage
'Adam's Orange'
'Aranályom'
'Brandywine'
'Cleopatre'
'Constitution'
'Delaware'
'Jivago'
'Kreta'
'Liberation'
'Losotho Lil'
'Mrs Tim Taylor'
'Orange Beauty'
'Orange Perfection'
'Orange Punch'
'Penn'
'Red Dazzler'
'Singapore Girl'
'Stadt Fellbach'
'Tango'
'Vera Cole'

Orange flowers with dark foliage
'Australia'
'Brighton Orange'
'Délibáb'
'General Eisenhower'
'Ingeborg'
'Intrigue'
'Liberté'
'Louis Cottin'
'Madame Angele Martin'
'Passionata'

'Roi Humbert'
'Saumur'
'Sémaphore'
'Südfunk'
'Verdi'
'Vermilion'
'Wyoming'

Pink flowers with green foliage
'Aida'
'Alberich'
'Angel Pink'
'Centenaire de Rozain-Boucharlat'
'China Doll'
'China Lady'
'Ehemanii'
'Favourite'
'French Plum'
'La Traviata'
'Liberty Cantaloupe'
'Liberty™ Coral Rose'
'Liberty™ Pink'
'Liberty™ Watermelon'
'Mrs Pierre du Pont'
'North Star™ Princess'
'Pallag Szépe'
'Perkeo'
'Prince Charmant'
'Rosenkavalier'
'Ruby Cole'
'Tropical Rose'

Pink flowers with dark foliage
'Champigny'
'Di Bartolo'
'Pink Futurity'
'Rose Futurity'

'Saladin'
'Shenandoah'
'Shining Pink'
'Zulu Princess'
'Zulu Queen'

Yellow flowers
'C. F. Cole'
'Chesapeake'
'Conestoga'
'Elma Cole'
'Felix Ragout'
'Golden Girl'
'Harvest Yellow'
'Independence'
'King City Gold'
'King Midas'
'Lenape'
'L. G. Cole'
'Liberty™ Keylime'
'North Star™ Desert
    Yellow'
'Petit Poucet'
'Pfitzer's Primrose
    Yellow'
'Richard Wallace'
'Rigoletto'
'Sémaphore'
'Striped Beauty'
'Yellow Futurity'

**Salmon and apricot
    flowers**
'Aida'
'Alberich'
'Ambrosia'
'Apricot Dream'
'Apricot Frost'
'Apricot Ice'
'Champion'
'Chinese Coral'
'City of Portland'

'Cole's Pale Superba'
'Extase'
'Gnom'
'Horn'
'King Hakon'
'La Bohème'
'La Gloire'
'Liberation'
'Louis Cayeux'
'Madame Angele
    Martin'
'Madame Paul
    Casaneuve'
'Marjorie Cole'
'Mrs Oklahoma'
'Nattie Cole'
'Nectarine'
'Peach Blush'
'Pfitzer's Salmon Pink'
'Princess Di'
'Tirol'

Near-white flowers
'Ambassadour'
'Begonia'
'Dondo'
'Eureka'
'Gran Canaria'
'Oiseau d'Or'

**Bicoloured, spotted
    or blotched
    flowers**
'African Scarlet
    Speckle'
'Cleopatra'
'Colibri'
'Cote d'Or'
'Dolly Gay'
'En Avant'
'Florence Vaughan'
'Gaiety'

'Glowing Embers'
'Heinrich Seidel'
'Italia'
'Journey's End'
'Lenape'
'Lippo's Kiwi'
'Lucifer'
'Mandarin Orange'
'Meyerbeer'
'Picasso'
'Rosemond Coles'
'Talisman'
'Taroudant'

Compact cultivars
'Alberich'
'Ambrosia'
'Angel Pink'
'Apricot Ice'
'Brandywine'
'Brilliant'
'Butterscotch'
'C. F. Cole'
'Chesapeake'
'China Doll'
'China Lass'
'Corsica'
'Empire'
Futurity Series
'Gnom'
'Gran Canaria'
'Horn'
'Journey's End'
'Kreta'
'Lemon Yellow'
'Louis Cottin'
'Lucifer'
'Madeira'
'Maggie'
'Merle Cole'
North Star Series™
'Orange Punch'

'Pallag Szépe'
'Petit Poucet'
'Pfitzer's Primrose
    Yellow'
'Pfitzer's Salmon Pink'
'Pink Sunburst'
'Puck'
'Roitelot'
'Südfunk'
'Sunny Delight'
'Tropical Rose'
'Valentine'

Small-flowered
'Cerise Davenport'
'Intrigue'
'Mystique'
'Orange Perfection'
'Panache'
'Passionata'
'Robert Kemp'
'Warzcewiczii'

Foliage
'Australia'
'Durban'
'Intrigue'
'Kansas City'
'Musifolia'
'Mystique'
'Pink Sunburst'
'Pretoria'
'Striped Beauty'

**Easy to obtain and
    grow**
'City of Portland'
'Lucifer'
'President'
'Richard Wallace'
'Strasbourg'
'Wyoming'

APPENDIX 6

FREQUENTLY ASKED QUESTIONS

Over the years that I have been growing cannas, exhibiting them at shows and corresponding with gardeners, I have been asked a number of questions quite regularly. These and their answers are listed below.

Will my canna flower this year? Yes, if planted in good time and, given good growing conditions, most cannas can be expected to flower in their first season.

Why doesn't my canna flower? The most common reason is poor growing conditions. Cannas are greedy and need plenty of water and food. They respond well to being divided; old clumps are less likely to flower.

Why did my canna die in winter? Canna rhizomes die if conditions are too cold, too wet or too dry. The most common cause of death in storage is desiccation caused by keeping the roots warm without sufficient moisture.

What causes the holes in my canna leaves? Early in the season, it is likely to be slugs; later, and higher up on the plant, caterpillars may cause damage.

How many divisions can I expect to get next year? Most cannas will divide into between 3 to 7 divisions, although the number is very variable according to the cultivar and the size of the clump.

What is the name of this canna? Naming of unlabelled cannas can be very difficult. Some identification of distinct cultivars is possible but it is never possible to tell whether a plant is just a 'look-alike' hybrid.

Will they grow outside in the British Isles? Yes, cannas will grow and thrive in most parts of Britain during the summer months but will die down to the ground as soon as the frosts appear.

Can cannas be grown from seed? Yes, cannas can easily be grown from seed but they rarely breed true so the results may be either exciting or disappointing.

Are cannas fussy about soil types? Cannas will grow in most soils that are well cultivated and reasonably rich (see p.39).

Do I have to dig them up at the end of the season? To be absolutely sure of overwintering cannas in a frosty climate, this is essential. However, many growers are willing to risk leaving them out, covered in a thick mulch. It's a gamble!

If I plant my cannas deep, will it protect the roots from the frost? Deep planting is likely to result in slow growth and poor flowering. It is better to use a deep mulch over the roots in winter.

Can you grow cannas in the shade? Yes, but there will be far fewer flowers, and foliage colour, especially with the darker-leaved types, will be poor.

Can you grow cannas as pot plants? Cannas make excellent conservatory plants in large pots or tubs but need good light. They will not succeed under poor light in the average house.

Will my canna be taller next year? Not really, because cannas reach a finite height when they flower and after that the stem dies down. Good growing conditions will, however, cause vigorous growth and extra height in a good season.

Can I take cuttings from cannas? No, not in the recognized sense of a stem cutting. However, people sometimes refer to a division as a 'cutting' (see p.55).

Can I bring cannas back from my holiday abroad? Small quantities of plants can legally be brought back from Europe. From outside Europe, plants must be properly prepared and accompanied by a Phytosanitary Certificate (see p.151).

Can I plant cannas directly in the garden as I don't have a greenhouse? Yes, but they must be planted later and they will be slower to grow and flower.

APPENDIX 7

PROBLEM NAMES

The following is a summary of most of the naming problems discussed elsewhere. In some cases there is an additional name that has crept in through common usage but is not validated. On occasions there are two or more validated names but the plants appear to be identical. In most cases, the likely correct name is listed first.

'Ambassador', 'Black Knight', 'Black Velvet', 'America', 'Liebesglut' – possibly synonymous

'Assaut', 'Hercule', 'Lafayette', 'Vainqueur' – possibly synonymous

'Bankok', 'Striped Beauty', Christ's Light', 'Nirvana', 'Minerva', 'King of Siam' – synonymous

'City of Portland', 'Orchid' – synonymous

'Cleopatra', 'Yellow Humbert' – synonymous

'Délibáb' – stocks very muddled

'Durban', 'Phasion', 'Tropicanna' – synonymous

'General Eisenhower', 'Paddy's Red' – very similar, neither validated

'King Humbert', 'Roi Humbert', 'Red King Humbert' – stocks very muddled

'Mrs Oklahoma', 'Miss Oklahoma', 'Los Angeles', 'Pink President' – synonymous

'Perkeo', 'Fatamorgana', 'Evening Star', 'Francis Berti' – synonymous

'Pretoria', 'Striatum', *malawiensis variegata*, 'Bengal Tiger', 'Panaché' – synonymous

'Richard Wallace', 'King Midas' – synonymous

'Stuttgart', 'Striata' – synonymous

'Tirol' – several forms available

'Wyoming', 'Professor Lorentz', 'Liberté' – probably the same

INDEX

ACKNOWLEDGEMENTS

Writing a book on a favourite subject is both fun and hard work, but is rarely done in isolation, and this one is no exception. My appreciation goes to the many people worldwide who have over the years encouraged me in my interest in cannas, who have generously swapped plants with me and who have given me access to their own research information.

Initially, I would like to thank Brian Halliwell, who gave me those first five cannas so many years ago and kindled that original interest. My appreciation goes to Philip McMillan Browse, who widened my eyes beyond our own United Kingdom boundaries by importing for me the first collection of cannas from France. I express my gratitude to Ed Snyder, Francis Ng, Jacky Fazio of Brooklyn Botanics and Tomasz Anisko of Longwood Gardens, and many others, for the plants they have generously sent me. Keith and Margaret Hayward must especially be mentioned for their generosity in sharing information and so many plants over the years.

Particular thanks must go to Jim Waddick, Stan Tyson, Kent Kelly, Mike Underwood and Scott Kunst, who have been remarkably patient with me over many months, while I was preparing my trip to the USA, and who were then so welcoming and hospitable during those memorable two weeks.

My thanks go to Jolene Snow of Horn's Canna Farm, Hayes Jackson and Bob Armstrong for information and advice. I acknowledge the contribution of Paul and Hiltje Maas on canna species. I especially recognize the research assistance from Ray Cooper, who provided long lists of canna references that yielded many gems of information, and Thomas Brown for his amazing archive on nineteenth-century cultivars.

Thanks to Joy Cooke for looking after and expanding the collection over several years. I acknowledge the support of Nottingham University in allowing me to grow my collection in Highfields Walled Garden and express my appreciation to Chris Price and his team for looking after them. (Sorry guys – there are now so many plants!)

Thanks also to my partner Philip for his patience and encouragement, while I have been writing this book.